Exploring/Teaching the Psychology of Women

SUNY Series in the Psychology of Women

Michele A. Paludi, Editor

Exploring/Teaching the Psychology of Women

A Manual of Resources

Michele A. Paludi

State University of New York Press

Published by
State University of New York Press, Albany

For information, address State University of New York
Press, State University Plaza, Albany, N.Y., 12246

Library of Congress Cataloging-in-Publication Data

Paludi, Michele Antoinette
    Exploring/teaching the psychologyof women : a manual of resources
/ Michele A. Paludi.
        p.   cm. — (SUNY series in the psychology of women)
    ISBN 0-88706-872-3. (pbk.)
    1. Women—Psychology—Study and teaching.   2. Women—Psyhology—Outlines,
syllabi,etc.   3. Women—Psychology—Study and teaching—Audio-visual aids.
    4. Women—Psychology—Bibliography.   I. Title.   II. Series.
HQ1206.P27   1990
155.6′33′07—dc19   88-6412
                                                                              CIP

10   9   8   7   6   5   4   3   2   1

In loving memory
of my mother,
Antoinette Rose Peccichio Paludi,
and my father,
Michael Anthony Paludi,
my most influential teachers
in the psychology of women,

I dedicate this book

to my friends and colleagues in
scholarship on women at Hunter College
who have demonstrated the cooperative
spirit Antoinette and Michael
wanted me to be a part of:

Joan Tronto

Darlene DeFour

Ros Petchesky

Dorothy O. Helly

Florence Denmark

Sue Rosenberg Zalk

Richard Barickman

Contents

Contents

Contents

Contents

Foreword

It is with great pleasure that I introduce, *Exploring/Teaching the Psychology of Women: A Manual of Resources*, edited by Michele A. Paludi, Associate Professor of Psychology and Women's Studies at Hunter College of the City University of New York. This work is part of the SUNY Series, The Psychology of Women.

The title of the book *Exploring/Teaching the Psychology of Women: A Manual of Resources* is especially appropriate. Manual, from the Latin, *manualis* is an adjective, meaning: of or pertaining to the hand or hands, done or performed with the hands. The title is important because by her personal "hands-on" exploration of the teaching of the psychology of women, Michele Paludi has given us much more than a theoretical treatise on the psychology of women. Instead, she has given us a rich compendium of resources which can be used by both students and instructors alike. Her work serves as a model of a feminist way of teaching and of learning which is applicable to teaching the psychology of women and which is also generalizable to enhancing the teaching of virtually any course.

Most of the work for this resource manual was completed during the two years in which the author was a Visiting Associate Professor of Psychology and Women's Studies at Hunter College. I had the enriching experience of knowing Michele during this book's inception, while I was Thomas Hunter Professor of Psychology at Hunter College. I am very proud to be one of the people to whom Michele, always generous in her acknowledgment of the assistance of others, has dedicated this book.

Through her personal path of exploration of the teaching of psychology of women, Paludi developed several small group experiential exercises, interpersonal activities, and process skills which incorporated feminist principles and values generated by her research into women's achievement and career development into the educational process. Specific pedagogical methods based on feminist values such as facilitating discussion, sharing leadership, and providing relevant resources are clearly presented in this manual. Instructors are given a series of experiential exercises, questions for debate, sample syllabi, references, organizations, and audio-visual material relevant to the content area of psychology of women. This manual provides resources concerning issues of achievement, development, life-style choices, sexuality, psychotherapy, communication, victimization, adjustment, and work.

Paludi is most successful in her ability to express to students and instructors alike the living link between feminist class content and process. When both students and instructors become increasingly self-aware, feminism facilitates new relationships and the content of this manual comes to life in the classroom and beyond it. Paludi accomplishes this feat by focusing on: life-stage concerns, feminist identity development, shared leadership in the learning process and integrating emotional and personal learning. For example, undergraduate students between the ages of 18 and 22 often express the view that problems of inequality in the areas of salary, law, power, and attitudes no longer exist. Many of these students have not experienced parenting, divorce, or job discrimination as yet. By comparison, older reentry students have often had these experiences and now question their relationship to societal values. This manual presents materials relevant to different life stage concerns and facilitates discussion to "bridge the awareness gap" so that high levels of interest from students of all ages are stimulated and maintained. Women of different ages are encouraged to assimilate information about the psychology of women at various life stages and to become aware of continued bias and discrimination. This manual provides exercises and topics for discussion which tend to draw out students' and instructors' personal experiences and enable them to form new observations based on a deeper understanding of life stage concerns which affect all women.

Another area in which this manual fosters the living link between feminist class content and process is that of feminist identity development. Typically, students are in a transitional development stage where they are seeking to define their own identity. The process of role experimentation is crucial to resolve the issue of self-definition. Role experimentation, or what Erikson called psychological moratorium, can occur in many different forms such as different jobs, changing one's college major, exploring various religions, etc. with the end product being the individual's definition of herself in society. This manual enhances the psychosocial moratorium by integrating feminist principles and making them come alive by providing students with a set of guest speakers who team teach the material. Via the process of team teaching, Paludi is able to illustrate the concept of "personal is political" to students. Quite simply, when a student is exposed to only one instructor's point of view, she may believe that if she agrees with it, she is just identifying with one person's point of view. Team teaching the psychology of women can provide students with a greater connection between their own experiences and those shared by many other women. This manual provides lists of topics, exercises to develop new interactional skills, and techniques designed to foster relationships between guest speakers and students in a variety of areas such as volunteer work and research experience. Exposure to a variety of feminist instructors contributes to students' growth, pursuit of career options, and to the development of feminist identity.

By illustrating the concept of shared leadership in the classroom, this manual serves as a model of feminist teaching which could enhance the learning process of any course. Specific techniques designed to enhance students' self-concept as participants in the learning process, such as the extinction of hierarchical arrangements, and use of several cofacilitators who are on a first name basis with the other participants, are presented. This dissemination of power and cooperative classroom structure, along with the elimination of tests and letter grades empowers students and usually results in their producing high quality work.

This manual also provides students and instructors with methods for integrating emotional and personal learning, resulting in greater congruence and enhanced self-esteem. Pedagogical techniques which foster self-expression in the classroom, including the expression of anger are encouraged. Permission to express and acknowledge anger is apparent. Methods for fostering the participants' ability to use the energy of their anger to produce individual and societal change are outlined. Techniques which enhance interpersonal communication skills, especially the use of "I" statements that express the participants feelings in relation to another's behavior expressed in operational, non-judgmental terms are effective in promoting constructive feedback, a supportive atmosphere, and an enhanced authenticity for all participants. This manual promotes discussion about a "continuum of feminism" and refutes the idea that there is "one kind" of feminist. Feminist pedagogy is brought to life with illustrations that discuss concerns relevant to both men and women. To be "pro-female" does not mean being "anti-male". Group behavior can sometimes differ in mixed vs. same-sex groups. Examples of reactions to male presence in the psychology of women classroom illustrate hierarchical forms of group process present in society which are often detrimental to women. The manual provides guidelines for establishing an empathic environment and reducing group hierarchy.

The integration of the fruits of women's studies programs with psychology has resulted in an increased awareness of class and racial as well as gender issues. Paludi noted that our model of female development has indeed shifted from that of the white middle class woman to encompass women of color. Thus, the information presented here is useful as feminist pedagogy as well as teaching history, development, and research methods relevant to people of color.

In summary, this book makes a definitive contribution as an invaluable resource for teaching and experiencing the psychology of women.

Florence L. Denmark, Ph.D.
Robert Scott Pace Professor
and Chair, Dept. of Psychology
Pace University

Preface

I am most grateful to my colleagues at Hunter College for their helpful suggestions and support: Dorothy O. Helly, Richard Barickman, Sue Rosenberg Zalk, Florence Denmark, Darlene DeFour, Joan Tronto, Eve Leoff, Mary Lefkarities, Ros Petchesky, Susan Lees, Marnia Lazreg.

My Women's Career Development Research Collective at Hunter also deserves recognition: Carole Ann Scott, Marc Grossman, Joni Kindermann, Judi Dovan, Don Grimm, Pamela Schneider, Meryl Zacker, Lorraine McKenney, Elizabeth Wilson-Anstey, Lisa Goldstein, Deborah Meyers, Deborah Dekelbaum.

I am thankful for the work done by the College of Continuing Studies at Kent State University for supporting my teaching of several courses on the psychology of women and gender roles, in addition to my chairing the First Biennial Meeting of the Midwestern Society for Feminist Studies. Many of the pedagogical techniques described in this resource manual were used in these courses and at the conference.

My colleagues who have discussed the teaching of the psychology of women with me deserve recognition: Kat Quina, Barbara Sholley, Chalsa Loo, Mary Roth Walsh, Deborah Belle, Patricia Arrendondo, Ellen Kashack, and Alice Collins, Darlene DeFour, Bea Krauss.

The conversation hours devoted to feminist instruction and scholarship I chaired at the American Psychological Association, Midwestern Society for Feminist Studies, Association for Women in Psychology, and American Educational Research Association provided me with much opportunity to learn strategies for feminist teaching. I thank each one of the participants in these conversation hours: Mary Roth Walsh, Virginia O'Leary, Irene Hanson Frieze, Janet Hyde, Nancy Henley, Barbara Gutek, Louise Fitzgerald, Sandy Shullman, Vivian Makosky, Nancy Benham, Marilee Niehoff, Patricia Rozee-Koker, Carole Garrison, Leonore Tiefer, Karen Maitland Schilling, Susan Basow, Joan Tronto, Mary Kite, Michael Stevenson, Carole Corcoran, Susan Hardin, Linda Subich, Virginia Valian, Darlene DeFour, Florence Denmark, Martha Banks, Nancy Betz, Margaret Matlin, and Bea Krauss.

I thank my colleagues who contributed exercises to this manual: Christine Sleight, Margaret Matlin, Jacquelynne Eccles, Andrea Parrot, Darlene DeFour, and Vivian Makosky.

I am most grateful to Lois Patton, Editor-in-Chief at SUNY Press, who helped shape the basic concept and style of this book, for her moral support: she kept me going! Collaborating with Lois provided me with much inspiration and hope.

Suzanne Siegel, my colleague at Hunter College, was invaluable as a library assistant.

I appreciate the assistance of several colleagues for their reviews of various sections of this manual: Margaret Matlin, Mary Koss, Florence Denmark, Christine Sleight.

A special note of appreciation goes to Nancy Walbek, my professor in the psychology of women at Union College and to Dee Graham and Edna Rawlings who invited me to be their teaching assistant in their course on the psychology of women at the University of Cincinnati. I am also appreciative of Tony Grasha for his graduate courses in the psychology of teaching. He also encouraged my pursuit of feminist teaching techniques.

I especially would like to thank students in my courses on the psychology of women at Hunter College for their insight, encouragement, and sage advice.

The following individuals who contributed sample syllabi for this manual are also thanked: Ellen Kimmel, Michael Stevenson, Carole Corcoran.

Introduction

When I was a graduate student in experimental psychology at the University of Cincinnati (1976–1980), I had the opportunity to teach a course entitled "A Practicum in Thinking." This course was designed to assist undergraduate students with a variety of thinking skills, including mnemonic devices, note taking, listening skills, verbal communication skills, and logical reasoning and hypothesis testing. As part of my responsibilities for this course, I developed several small group experiential exercises, interpersonal activities, and process skills. My in-class participation consisted mostly of facilitating discussion, giving students tasks to try shared leadership, and providing resources in the form of organizations, popular books and articles, reference material, and additional experiential exercises. On the teaching evaluations for this course several students remarked that they had learned as much or more from the process of the course—its hidden curriculum—as they did from its explicit content. I realized for the first time that the greater the congruence between the content and process of a course, the more consistent students' learning could be. I also learned that the greater this congruence was, the happier I was with teaching.

I unfortunately wasn't able to continue with facilitating small groups courses at the undergraduate level when, as a faculty member at Kent State University, I was assigned large auditorium sections of developmental psychology, statistics, and adolescent psychology. I mostly lectured in these courses and tried my very best to get students to analyze and think about others' theories and ideas as well as to develop their own theories. The first time I taught a course on the psychology of women (actually it was called "The Development of Sex Role and Identity") it was in a large lecture hall (approximately 135 seats). Giving information to these students was the easiest part of teaching. However, I did not feel happy with my performance despite the kudos on teaching evaluations. The congruence between course content and process that was present in my small groups courses was absent. The real challenge of teaching skills to students and inspiring an interest that would help them understand the course content more fully was absent. And, I believed the students were not receiving enough self-awareness to take that understanding with them throughout their lives. In short, I believed the feminist values on which I was basing my research into women's achievement and career development was not being expressed in my classroom performance. I thus decided to restructure the "hidden curriculum" of my courses, especially the course on the psychology of women, in order to better reflect feminist principles. I wanted feminism to facilitate new relationships between people; the classroom seemed to be an important place for this to occur.

1

Identical concerns were being raised at a similar time by Irene Hanson Frieze, in her editorial in the April, 1984 Division 35 (Psychology of Women) of the American Psychological Association Newsletter. Spurred by this editorial, Mary Roth Walsh organized and chaired several conversation hours devoted to curriculum revisions. I was fortunate to participate in two of these conversation hours inasmuch as they gave me an opportunity to discuss teaching problems and techniques in a supportive environment.

The culmination of my translating feminist values into educational praxis in the psychology of women course is presented in this resource manual. In this volume I present educational processes which reflect feminist principles as I have interpreted them. I gave examples of how I use these methods in the courses I have taught at Kent State University and Hunter College. Sample syllabi, outlines, references, audio-visual material, organizations, discussion questions, and experiential exercises are also presented here according to the content area typically covered in psychology of women courses: achievement, sexuality, health, adjustment, psychotherapy, communication, victimization, methodology, life-style choices, work, development. Syllabi of courses in the psychology of women from several colleagues enhance this resource manual. Resources from colleagues who responded to a survey I compiled (presented at the end of this introduction) are also included.

What I have found most important is to express to the students the relationship between the feminist class content and process. The methods I use to accomplish this goal have been published and presented elsewhere (see Paludi, 1985; 1986a, b) and will be summarized here with respect to the following issues: life-stage concerns, feminist identity development, shared leadership in the classroom, cooperative structures, and incorporating emotional/ personal learning.

The goals I had in mind for transforming the psychology of women course centered around the following feminist frameworks (*e.g., Lord, 1982*).

1. The course should be a laboratory of feminist principles.

2. The traditional patriarchal teaching-learning model is dysfunctional in the development of healthy women and men.

3. Every individual in the class is a potential teaching resource.

4. Integration is imperative for the development of healthy, whole women and men. Therefore, the course should foster mind/body integration as well as the integration of ideas and behavior, and thoughts and feelings.

5. Effective human behavior in social interactions and within social systems is related to understanding the relationship between the personal and the political.

6. A women's studies course should deal with women only and treat women as the norm.

7. If at all possible, the primary coordinators of the course should be women.

8. The subjective, personal experience of women and men is valid and important.

9. The student should ultimately assume responsibility for her or his own learning and growth.

10. Cooperation among students in pursuing learning objectives creates a more positive learning climate than does competition; cooperative learning is fostered through the use of criterion-referenced rather than a norm-referenced evaluation system.

11. Providing vehicles outside the class through which students can deal with personal feelings and frustrations (such as journals, dyads, assertiveness training, and growth groups) enhances the quality of class distinction.

12. The generic use of terms such as woman and the female pronouns to refer to humans is an effective teaching-learning tool.

13. Both men and women should be exposed to and have an understanding of the course material. However, a structure must be provided which allows women to meet with women and men with men for a significant portion of the time.

Life-stage concern

One common problem reported by instructors of the courses in the psychology of women concerns students' beliefs that problems of inequality in salary, politics, business, attitudes, and law have all been solved. I, too, have experienced students less willing to accept the presence of discrimination and bias in work, academia, and the family. Women students especially voiced their opinion that marrying an accommodating husband would be the sole factor needed in order to "have it all." Upon closer examination, I learned that the conservatism concerned life events with which late adolescents/early adulthood students have not yet mastered or dealt, *e.g.*, menopause, parenting, divorce, job discrimination. Reentry students, unlike undergraduates between the ages of 18 and 22, have defined adulthood, *e.g.*, questions of their relationship to the existing society, lifestyles, vocation.

With this awareness, I developed materials relevant to students' life-stage

3

that served to maintain high levels of interest as well as to illustrate the continued bias and discriminatory practices. Exercises and topics for discussion can draw from personal experience as well as new observation to encourage the assimilation of information about the psychology of women. This resource manual contains sample films, references, popular books, organizations, and experiential exercises I have used in teaching the psychology of women, taking into account students' life-stage.

Feminist identity development

The majority of students who participate in courses on the psychology of women (as well as in other courses) are typically in a transitional phase of their development in which they are preoccupied with questions about their essential character that will satisfy their longing for self-definition (Erikson, 1959; Newman and Newman, 1984). The central process through which individuals resolve this identity issue is role experimentation. This process of role experimentation or psychological moratorium (Erikson, 1959)) may take several forms (*e.g.,* part time jobs, changing the college area of specialization, dating, investigating religious and political theories, developing a point of view about feminism), and results in the individuals' personal conception of how they fit into society.

One way I have incorporated the psychosocial moratorium into courses on the psychology of women has been to devise experiential exercises and topics for discussion that draw from personal experiences. Other recommendations include: (a) having students conduct empirical research on a topic of their choice (Riger, 1978; 1979); (b) adopting a nonhierarchical strategy in which the instructor is a facilitator of discussion, not an authority (Freedman, Golub, & Krauss, 1982; Howe, 1975); (c) dividing the class into same-sex discussion groups (Piliavin and Martin, 1976; Thorne and Henley, 1975, and; (d) evaluating book authors' feminist positions (Sholley, 1986).

One additional effective translation of the psychosocial moratorium concerns providing students with a set of instructors or guest speakers who team teach the material. Exposure to a variety of women can contribute to students' growth, self-concept development, self-definition in terms of feminism, and pursuit of career options (Faunce, 1985; Wallston *et al.,* 1978).

Feminist instructors have considerable ability to empathize with women students ability to empathize with women students because of shared experiences of being a woman in this culture as well as increased sensitivity to women's issues (Faunce, 1985). Furthermore, team-teaching the psychology of women course emphasizes the "personal is political" concept: that women's experiences are shared by every woman and are therefore political. When students are exposed to only one instructor in this course, they may not see the connection between their own (or of their women friends') experiences as individual women and those that happen to all women. Team-teaching the psychology of women course can provide students with validation for their own experiences, learning new interactional skills, and affirming individual perceptions of experience. An interdisciplinary perspective also challenges the emphasis on specialized knowledge in a specialty area.

I have adopted these pedagogical techniques in several classes. With permission from the guest speakers, I distribute a list of their names to the students, who are encouraged to contact them for further information and possible volunteer work or research experience. One adoption of these techniques to assist students in their feminist identity development has been through continuing education courses sponsored by the College of Continuing Studies at Kent State University. The courses, entitled "Women: Issues and Images: A Series of Lectures and Discussion," met weekly for two hours. Co-facilitators have been women faculty, students, administrators, and emeritus professors. They have ranged in age from 25 to 80. Each week a co-facilitator presented information on a particular topic with which she is familiar (because of research, teaching, and/or applied focus). Titles of presentations given during the spring and fall, 1986 series were the following:

Spring, 1986

The new psychology of women: From rocking the cradle to rocking the boat

Tarnishing the ivory tower: Gender and sexual harassment

Outrageous acts and everyday seductions: Date rape on college campuses

Counseling issues with minority women

Women and sexuality: Truths and fallacies

Black women: Images in perspective

Do women fear success?

Third World women

Women, middle age, and aging: Reactions to biological aspects of aging

Problems of older aged women

Single women: Leisure activities

Anorexia and bulimia: Indices of role strain

Future of women

Fall, 1986

Women's verbal and nonverbal communication styles

Women and day care

Women in the Bible

Women's friendships with mothers and others

Single mothers

Women and work

Battered women

Women and drugs

Providers of women's health care: Witches, nurses, and midwives

Participants had the option for registering for any or all sessions each time the series was offered. Within each session, co-facilitators used experiential exercises and/or cited research findings relevant to the participants' life-stage. Furthermore, co-facilitators provided participants with reference material related to the issue to be discussed. In addition, I set up a "resource table" on which were displayed articles from popular professional journals, pamphlets, and books related to the evening's topic for discussion. participants were given the opportunity to browse through the material prior to and after the presentation. They were encouraged to borrow material. Copies of public announcements were provided. I have set up similar resource tables in my large sections of the psychology of women courses as well. Lists of materials I have used in this regard are presented in this manual.

The woman focus of the series has been important in preventing women from backing off from their own experiences. Very little, if any, of the discussions each week was devoted to comparing women with men in order to avoid the "who's got it worse" game (Faunce, 1985). Furthermore, there was tremendous support value of having co-facilitators. Most of them attended most or all of the sessions as participants; this served to ease the isolation that may occur when only one individual teaches the psychology of women course (Carmen and Driver, 1982). The team teaching approach encourages experimentation with different expressions of feminism for the co-facilitators as well as the other participants.

Shared leadership in the classroom

When co-taught by several instructors or guest speakers, the psychology of women course allows individuals the freedom from the expectations of role performance. Their experimentation with new feminist roles, values, and belief systems may result in a personal conception of how they fit into feminist aspects of their culture. Furthermore, power is disseminated in several ways: no syllabus is distributed, no tests or papers or letter grades (except for "satisfactory") are assigned. Co-facilitators are referred to by their first names as are participants; hierarchical arrangements are eliminated. The co-facilitators and participants are both learners and experts; knowledge and experience is shared. At the beginning of each session, participants are asked to share announcements, celebrations, and concerns with all those present.

I have tried to disseminate power in my more traditional courses offered through the college or university. Some of these techniques include the following:

1. Arranging the seats in a circle. I make sure I rotate my own seat each class period so no one part of the circle is identified as being related to leadership In large lecturc halls I frequently restructure the room so students can sit on desks, tables, and floors so they can see each other.

2. Students' participation in structuring the course. I take primary responsibility for structuring my courses; however on the first day of class, I ask students what they initially like about the class, what they are uncertain about, what they would like changed (*e.g.*, number of exams, length of paper) and topics they want to discuss that are not on the syllabus. I ask each student to list for the class one thing they like and one thing they want some clarification about. I post these responses on the chalkboard for all participants to see. Modifications in the course requirements have been made in order to meet the participants' needs.

3. Feedback about the course content and process. Throughout the semester I periodically ask participants for feedback about the course topics and the process. For example, when I administer in-class exams, I ask participants to anonymously tell me (on the last sheet in the exam booklet that is ripped off and handed in independently of the exam) the concerns they had with my wording of the questions, format of the exam, material covered and not covered, study guide, review sessions. I then modify the subsequent exams taking participants' suggestions into account.

   I frequently "data collect" aloud. I ask participants to take 2–3 minutes to think about what they've learned after the discussion, what is hindering them from meeting their goal in the course, etc. When this data collection is done anonymously (frequently the case toward the beginning of the course when we are not familiar with on another and are working toward developing a sense of trust) I summarize the responses and report back to the participants at the next session. We try to work through the problem areas and make needed changes. Throughout this processing, considerable information about the psychology of women in terms of leadership styles, direct confrontation *vs.* gossiping, etc. can be discussed.

4. Course evaluations. In addition to the department course evaluation (typically quantitative in nature) I distribute an open-ended survey asking participants to comment on a variety of issues running the gamut from my effectiveness as a facilitator of a group to what they could have done differently to have made the course more enjoyable for them. I summarize participants' responses to these survey items on the final day of the class when we spend the session processing the course.

Of course, I am probably still perceived as having more power than the other participants. This seems to be especially the case in introductory psychology of women courses. Upper division and graduate students often are more receptive to nonhierarchical structures and reciprocity. Grading and evaluation issues still are more common areas of concern for undergraduate students. For grading purposes, I assign point for the completion of each course requirement. Exams and research proposals or papers are usually based on 100 points, experiential exercises or essay questions usually on 25. I strive to create an atmosphere that is free of competition throughout the entire teaching process, especially the evaluation I do not grade on a curve, and 90 percent of the total possible points is equivalent to an "A,", 80 percent a B, and so on.

I return each essay, exam, on paper to the participant with extensive comments about their integration of the material, organization, writing style, etc. I usually place the to-be-returned items on a table in the classroom in alphabetical order or in two piles: last names beginning with A-L and M-Z. Participants collect their papers either prior to or after the class session. I do not post any summary statistics about the participants' performance as a group.

Sometimes a pass/fail option has been available to me. I have found students to commend this pass/fail system and do high quality work.

Cooperative structures

Throughout our discussions in the classes on the psychology of women, I stress the connectedness of women, how it is undermined by the male power structure, and how women can be the best of friends and not the worst of enemies. In classes I attempt to make this statement nonverbally as well through the development of an atmosphere of mutual trust, respect, and community in our classroom. Many of the pedagogical techniques I have described thus far meet this goal of mine, *e.g.,* giving participants tasks to try shared leadership, democratic processes involved in course structure, grading, and exam preparation. Additional expressions of cooperative structures in the classroom include the following:

1. Breaking the classes into small discussion groups or "fishbowls" with an outer and an inner group. The inner group discusses the issue for 10–15 minutes. Students in the outer group are given 5–10 minutes at the end to make comments.

2. Assigning cooperative rather than independent term papers or research proposals.

3. Having "Women's Studies Day" or "The Psychology of Women Day" two or three times during the semester where participants bring articles, books, photos, films, posters, etc. they believe express feminist philosophy and practice. We integrate poetry (written by the participants themselves) as

well as women's music into these sessions. Participants are encouraged to bring friends with them and spend the class session browsing through the material and talking with other women. I usually bring pamphlets about the women's studies courses and certificate available to them as well as upper division women's studies students who can give some first-hand accounts of the courses and programs. These sessions have been successful network and community builders and work quite well in small as well as large classes.

4. When research proposals or term papers have been assigned I set up a mock "Psychology of Women" Conference at the end of the semester in which participants set their papers on display and are available for questions and answers (for large classes) or present a 10–15 minute summary of their papers (seminar classes). I complete the conference-like atmosphere for the class period(s) by providing students with name tags and brochures that lists all the participants' names and titles of their papers.

   Approximately one month before the papers are due I devoted class time to having participants discuss their ideas for their papers. After each participant concludes the brief presentation, I ask the other students to make suggestions in the form of possible reference material, organization of issues and feminist methodologies (for research proposals in graduate seminars).

5. Participants are encouraged to share personal and academic support information with the entire class. They may do this through handouts, writing announcements on the chalkboard, or orally presenting the information. In several classes, student support groups have been set up to help each other better understand feminist philosophy and its practice in their lives. These groups have often reported to the large group about their experiences.

6. Festive procedures like the "Psychology of Women Day" are good networking builders. These have included refreshments during class sessions and a pot-luck supper at the end of the semester.

7. When I have chaired departmental colloquia and local conferences (*e.g.*, Midwestern Society for Research in Life-Span Development and Midwestern Society for Feminist Studies) I have arranged for students to hear the presentations and meet the speakers informally.

Integration of emotional/personal learning

Since one of my goals in courses on the psychology of women is to have students integrate the course content into their daily lives, I spend a considerable amount of class time devoted to affective learning. Here are some of my common teaching techniques.

Journal writing.

Each participant is asked to analyze the readings, class presentations, and discussions and relate them to their personal experiences. Throughout the semester we devote a class session to sharing information form our journals (I usually keep one too). This technique helps participants to gain more confidence in their perceptions and evaluations and helps them trust their feelings.

Experiential exercises

These encourage the expression of feelings as well as integrate cognitive and affective learning. For example, in discussing the literature on women's achievement, I discuss why students choose or do not choose to take certain courses, *e.g.*, math. I have used Jacquelynne Eccles' model of academic course choice (Meese, *et al.*, 1982) to indicate to students how girls' and women's expectations and values may be shaped so that they do not take math courses in high school and college. More specifically, I have asked students to trace through the model for themselves, in order to see whether it predicts why they did or did not continue taking math courses in college (Hyde, 1985). Within the same unit I have asked students (typically reentry students) TO WRITE A 3–5 page paper describing an organization to which they belong (*e.g., PTA, NOW, Church groups) in terms of its purpose, sex ratio, ethnic and age composition, and success.*

Introspective, autobiographies

I have occasionally asked students to write an autobiographical account of their own gender-role socialization and its development, integrating it with theory and research discussed in class (adapted from Hyde, 1980). Because this assignment is one in which confidential information may be discussed, students' papers are assigned a code number, with no name. For those students who may be uncomfortable with such an assignment, an alternative that they may choose is to complete an analysis of a play or popular book character of their choice. The power of themes in the books and plays relate to students' experiences, important insights emerge from a discussion of these themes. Reading and commenting on these analyses requires considerable time and sensitivity; the value to students has always been significant.

Research proposals

In graduate seminars on the psychology of women I ask students to become acquainted with one aspect of the field by writing a proposal for research.

Students present a summary of their proposal and reference lists to other participants in the class.

Emotionally-laden topics

Several issues in the psychology of women (*e.g.*, lesbian relationships, racial, class, and ethnic distinctiveness) have created class sessions that have been emotionally charged arenas. In addition, many of the students who participate in introductory courses on women's studies and the psychology of women have never encountered feminist philosophy in prior courses. They may have no one at home or in their dorm with whom to discuss the class content; they may be seen as rocking the boat and may be laughed at and/or called derogatory names because of their association with women's studies and feminism. I therefore believe that the classroom needs to become a place where women can feel good about themselves and other women without the fear of being laughed at, considered "unfeminine," etc. Pedagogical techniques such as the ones described here have had the power to replace self-doubt with certainty, low self-esteem with self-respect and caring. Expressions of anger in the classroom sometimes stem from students realizing they may not be living their lives according to feminist principles; they may also feel their voice as a woman of Color is not being heard. Students may, as a result, fail to attend class regularly, play devil's advocate in each session and/or attempt to take leadership in the classroom. Often angry students arrive late, slam the classroom door shut, disrupt several students in nearby seats, and express other nonverbal signs of anger. Very commonly, manifestations of anger in the classroom become fixed on the instructor because of her expressions of feminism as she interprets them. All of these experiences have happened to me when facilitating the psychology of women courses. I have learned (emotionally painfully) to permit the acknowledgement of the anger and claiming the anger as well as directing the participants to express the energy tied into the anger toward individual and social change. In order to meet this goal I have devoted class time to interpersonal communication skills, especially the use of "I" statements, *e.g.*, "I feel _____ when you _____ because of _____. This technique has helped participants (myself included) give constructive feedback in a supportive atmosphere. I believe such communication skills have helped produce a more honest classroom.

Occasionally I have experienced students' anger fixing itself on other students. This has manifested itself in directing homophobic and racist remarks toward other women in the classroom. I have translated these comments into discussion about a "continuum of feminism" that there is not one kind of feminist. In addition, devoting class time to how to argue with ideas rather than people has been helpful.

When men have been present in the classroom such expressions of anger have taken the form of women aligning themselves with the outspoken men against other women in the class. I have directly intervened in such discussions, labeled the behavior and have tried to show how the behavior parallels what occurs to women in business meetings, court cases involving sex discrimination, and family decision making. This experience provides good examples for discussing nonverbal gestures of power, dominance, and submissiveness.

One example of such experiences occurred during the orientation class of an introductory course in women's studies I facilitated. After a description of the course content and process and a discussion of the syllabus, I asked each participant in the class to introduce themselves and tell the class something they hoped to learn from and discuss in the course. As typically happens, participants shared their experiences as reentry students, newly married or divorced, employed mothers, as a women's studies major, and so on. In this particular class, there were 51 women and 1 man. The man came to the first class 20 minutes after I had begun and failed to remove his earphones for the duration of my presentation and the other participants' comments. When it became his turn to introduce himself to the group, he promptly announced that more men should take this class, that there was too much of a women's perspective represented in the class and that his role in the class would be to tell women what men really want from women. I decided to initially ignore these comments until all participants had an opportunity to share their names and experiences. At first I didn't want to stop the class process and focus for a lengthy period of time on the only man's behavior. However, I quickly changed my mind when, following this man's comments, three of the women sitting near him began applauding his comments. I quickly intervened and pointed out that no applause was offered to any of the 34 women who also shared experiences (which included a rape, incest, problems with immigration, custody battle, and reentry status). I pointed out that the women's comments were relatively ignored, but the man's was applauded. I demanded that a round of applause be given to the women as well. I then described this information in the next class: feminist pedagogy, all women's classes, and the way in which women are inhibited by male presence, contributing to hierarchical forms seen in the larger society, which are detrimental to women (see Women's Studies College, State University of New York at Buffalo, 1983).

Of course my behavior was labeled by some participants as "anti-male." In fact, one of the most difficult concepts with which participants seem to deal concerns the point that being "pro-female" does not mean being "anti-male." I have found discussing gender role transcendence (*e.g.,* Parsons and Bryan, 1978; Rebecca, Hefner, and Olenshansky, 1976) to be helpful in this regard. This discussion, however, needs to be held several times throughout the semester in order for participants to see connections between their own experiences and transcendence.

A great deal of anger in my courses on the psychology of women has been generated by my presentations and the assigned readings. I have learned to ensure that the textbooks and readings for the class need to be read and discussed from the very beginning; participants may fail to do the assigned readings and assume the class presentations are based on my own idiosyncrasies. In the last few years I have felt I have been the bearer of bad news: subtle discrimination in the workplace, the myth of the Superwoman concept and having it all, etc. I do believe, however, it is my responsibility to tell students (emotionally and intellectually) the truth and not to protect them from awful realities. I want women to know that when discrimination occurs to them they are not at fault; that the onus for change is not on themselves. I hope this sharing of the emotional impact on students will help women to trust their own experiences and not impose self-silence and shame. I also believe it is important for women to see how other women have handled their anger and victimized and have become survivors. It is this developmental process I believe will ensure women working together and continuing to work for social change.

One related issue with which I have struggled concerns the amount of self-disclosure in and out of the classroom setting. I have shared many personal experiences, including my upbringing in an Italian-American working class family, my research projects, my traveling and participation at conferences. In my office I have prominently displayed photographs of my family, friends, and their children. This bulletin board of photographs elicits a great deal of questions about my life—both personal and professional. I believe it is important to tell participants who I am. Participants have commented on teaching evaluations that they thought my self-disclosure humanized the classroom. While I believe self-disclosure is positive, I have learned that there are some limitations to it. For example, participants may be alienated by self-disclosure on the part of the facilitator. I have found this to occur among individuals with no prior experience with feminist pedagogy. Facilitators who self-disclose may invite anger, hostilities, passions, infatuations.

I have found that my self-disclosure gives me the opportunity to reduce the student-professor hierarchy. I have also found that participants interpret my self-disclosure as a way to bring about social change. I am using my position to transcend stereotypes. I have frequently disclosed issues with which I am still struggling, *e.g.*, all-women's classes for women's studies classes. Writings by Beck (1983) have proved useful to me in this respect.

I have also learned to accept forms of appreciation from participants in the class. I have been given gifts as tokens of gratitude, been invited to after-class coffee hours and dinner, and I have been hugged. It took me some time to feel comfortable with these expressions; I initially was concerned about my getting "too close."

Women who have given me gifts were telling me in nonverbal ways how much I empowered them. This especially has been the case with reentry women. I realized my verbal and nonverbal communication, of rejecting their gifts was in many ways invalidating them. I now say "thank you" and feel more at ease. It was hard for me to receive from these women; but in so doing, I was denying their wish to give.

Concluding Remarks

I believe the pedagogical techniques I have outlined here help to demystify the hidden curriculum of the psychology of women course. Students also learn how to analyze their experiences outside of the classroom for underlying sexist and feminist principles. I hope the techniques outlined here will help foster women's development of a feminist identity according to the model proposed by Downing and Rousch (1985):

Stage I: *Passive Acceptance:* Beliefs that discrimination no longer is present; traditional roles are advantageous.

Stage II: *Revelation:* Open questioning of self and gender = role identity because of discrimination; feelings of anger and guilt.

Stage III: *Embeddedness-Emanation:* Connectedness with women; affirming new identity; cautious interaction with men.

Stage IV: *Synthesis:* Authentic and positive feminist identity: gender role transcendence.

Stage V: *Active Commitment:* Consolidation of feminist identity; commitment to meaningful action; to a nonsexist world.

I have described this model at the beginning of the class, and have used each of the stages as discussion topics throughout the course. Participants have found this particularly useful charting their experiences and feelings with topics of the course. Certain course topics contribute to more anger and guilt, *e.g.*, incest, rape, sexual and gender harassment, and mate abuse. In any given semester, I have had at least one-third of the women come to talk with me privately and/or discuss with the entire class their experiences with victimization. I have found it very helpful to distribute to all participants a list of organizations dealing with victimization of women. I have also found it helpful to give the names and phone numbers of academic and personal counselors at the college or university. I have encouraged women to meet with these counselors and discuss course content. I have included the names and addresses of a variety of organizations in this manual.

Feminist pedagogy allows us to use what we know as women to transform the classroom, a traditionally male-defined domain. There are many rewards in the feminist classroom. It has been exciting for me to be a part of a place where women's lives are changing. It is good to teach the psychology of women and work with women on these issues. However, feminist teaching can create a loneliness and isolation from one's colleagues. I therefore recommend support groups for feminist instructors of the psychology of women course. Mary Roth Walsh has developed a network of instructors of these courses. I too have organized several discussion sessions at national conventions surrounding surviving as a feminist instructor. Individuals who are willing to discuss the issues they do battle with because of their feminist pedagogy are listed in this manual in Chapter 1. The Association for Women in Psychology has also published a directory of members who can serve as resource persons. Information may also be obtained from the American Psychological Association's Women's Program Office.

I hope this resource manual will produce further dialogue. I would like to see this manual extend to instructors' as well as students' development. Feminist education suggests we enter into dialogues with other faculty as well as students, learning with them in a cooperative spirit. I look forward to hearing from you about your own feminist pedagogical techniques.

MICHELE A. PALUDI

References

Beck, E.T. (1983). "Self-disclosure and the commitment to social change." In C. Bunch and S. Pollack (Eds.), *Learning Our way: Essays in Feminist Education.* Trumansburg, NY: The Crossing Press.

Carmen, E., and Driver, F. (1983). "Teaching women's studies: Values in conflict." *Psychology of Women Quarterly, 7,* 81–95.

Downing, N.E. and Rousch, K.L. (1985). "From passive acceptance to active commitment: A model of feminist identity development for women." *The Counseling Psychologist, 13,* 695–709.

Erikson, E.H. (1959). "The problem of ego identity." *Psychological Issues, 1,* 101–164.

Faunce, P. (1985). "Teaching feminist therapies: Integrating feminist therapy, pedagogy, and scholarship." In L.B. Rosewater and L.E.A. Walker (Eds.), *Handbook of Feminist Therapy: Women's Issues in Psychotherapy.* New York: Springer.

Freedman, R.J., Golub, S., and Krauss, B. (1982). "Mainstreaming the psychology of women into the core curriculum." *Teaching of Psychology, 9,* 165–168.

Howe, F. (Ed.) 1975). *Women and the Power to Change.* New York: McGraw-Hill.

Hyde, J.S. (1980). *Instructors' Guide for Half the Human Experience.* Lexington, Mass.: Heath.

Hyde, J.S. (1985). *Half the Human Experience: The Psychology of Women.* Lexington, Mass.: Heath.

Lord, S.B. (1982). "Research on teaching the psychology of women." *Psychology of Women Quarterly, 7,* 96–104.

Meece, J., Eccles-Parsons, J., Kaczala, C.M., Goff, S.B., and Futterman, R. (1982). "Sex differences in math achievement: Toward a model of academic choice." *Psychological Bulletin, 91,* 324–348.

Newman, B.M., and Newman, P.R. (1984). *Development Through Life.* Homewood, IL: Dorsey.

Paludi, M.A. (1985, October). "Teaching the new psychology of women:

Life-stage concerns." Presentation at the American Education Research Association Special Interest Group on Research on Women and Education, Boston, MA.

Paludi, M.A. (1986a). "Teaching the psychology of gender roles: Some life-stage considerations." *Teaching of Psychology, 13,* 133–138.

Paludi, M.A. (1986b). "Teaching the psychology of women: Developmental considerations." Paper presented at the Annual Meeting of the Association for Women in Psychology, Denver, CO.

Parsons, J.E., and Bryan, J. (1978). *Adolescence: Gateway to Androgyny.* Michigan Occasional Paper. No. VIII.

Piliavin, J.A., and Martin, R.R. (1976). "The effects of sex composition of groups on style of social interaction." Reported in Deaux, K. *The Behavior of Women and Men.* Monterey, Calif.: Brooks/Cole.

Rebecca, M., Hefner, R., and Olenshansky, B. (1976). "A model of sex role transcendence." *Journal of Social Issues, 32,* 197–206.

Riger, S. (1978). "A technique for teaching the psychology of women: Content analysis." *Teaching of Psychology, 5,* 221–223.

Riger, S. (1979). "On teaching the psychology of women." *Teaching of Psychology, 6,* 113–114.

Sholley, B. (1986). "Value of book discussions in a psychology of women course." *Teaching of Psychology, 13,* 151–153.

Thorne, B., and Henley, N. (1975). *Language and Sex: Difference and Dominance.* Rowley, Mass.: Newbury House.

Wallston, B., Cheronis, J., Czirr, R., Edwards, S., and Russo, A. (1978, March). "Role models for professional women." Paper presented at the meeting of the Association for Women in Psychology, Pittsburgh, PA.

Women's Studies College, State University of New York at Buffalo (1983). "All women classes and the struggle for women's liberation." In C. Bunch and S. Pollack (Eds.), *Learning Our Way: Essays in Feminist Education.* Trumansburg, NY: The Crossing Press.

Survey of Issues Related to Teaching the Psychology of Women Course

1. What is the name of the course on the psychology of women that you teach (or have taught)?

2. Is this an undergraduate course or a graduate course or both? Please circle the appropriate response:

   1 undergraduate   2 graduate   3 both

3. What text(s) do you use (have you used) in this course:

4. What is the format for this course: Please circle the appropriate response:

   1 lecture   2 lecture with discussion   3 discussion

   4 other   (explain: _____)

5. Please list the typical requirements (e.g., tests, papers) for this course:

6. Have you had success in showing films in this course? If yes, please list 2–3 of the most popular ones:

7. Please briefly describe your techniques for dealing with personal/ emotional learning in the classroom.

8. What readings do you use for discussing the psychology of women of color?

9. Please briefly describe your grading system.

10. What topics (if any) do you find students having the most difficult time in discussing?

11. Do you typically have men taking the course? If yes, what are some of the issues involved in their presence in the classroom?

12. Please list some of the issues you have had to deal with as the instructor of this course (e.g., perceptions of power, devaluation of competency).

13. Have you had the opportunity to co-teach the psychology of women course?
    Please circle the appropriate response:

    1 Yes   2 No

    What are some of your thoughts on co-teaching this course?

14. How have you handled the conservatism of the students in the class?

15. List some of the ways you handle sexist comments from the students.

16. List some of the ways you handle racist comments.

17. How do you handle homophobic comments in the classroom?

18. Here are some of the topics traditionally covered in a psychology of women course. Please indicate (by placing checkmarks) whether you cover each topic in your course.

topic	lecture	film	reading	other (explain)
research methodology	_____	_____	_____	_____
theories of female personality	_____	_____	_____	_____
women's health	_____	_____	_____	_____
developmental issues in adolescence	_____	_____	_____	_____
developmental issues in middle age	_____	_____	_____	_____
developmental issues in older adulthood	_____	_____	_____	_____
lesbian relationships	_____	_____	_____	_____
bisexual relationships	_____	_____	_____	
AIDS	_____	_____	_____	_____
mental health and adjustment	_____	_____	_____	_____

feminist therapies   _____   _____   _____   _____

marriage   _____   _____   _____   _____

divorce   _____   _____   _____   _____

voluntary childlessness   _____   _____   _____   _____

remaining single   _____   _____   _____   _____

widowhood   _____   _____   _____   _____

single mothers   _____   _____   _____   _____

women and disabilities   _____   _____   _____   _____

victimization issues   _____   _____   _____   _____

cultural issues   _____   _____   _____   _____

history of the field of
psychology of women   _____   _____   _____   _____

stereotypes and
prejudice   _____   _____   _____   _____

cyclicity   _____   _____   _____   _____

women and sexuality   _____   _____   _____   _____

women's friendships   _____   _____   _____   _____

women and achievement   _____   _____   _____   _____

career development   _____   _____   _____   _____

women and work   _____   _____   _____   _____

leadership and power   _____   _____   _____   _____

communication styles   _____   _____   _____   _____

Other: write in

19. Are you:

    1 Female   2 Male

20. Your race:_____

21. Of what academic department are you a member?_____

22. Are you a:

    1 lecturer   2 adjunct   3 instructor   4 Assistant professor
    5 associate professor   6 full professor   7 graduate student   8 other
    (explain):_____

23. How many times a year is this course offered:_____

24. Please briefly describe the typical make-up of the participants in your classes—e.g., age, race, sex, class size.

25. Briefly describe the reasons students take this course.

26. Is this course cross-listed with the women's studies program?

    1 Yes   2 No

27. Have you integrated the material from this course into other courses you teach?

    1 Yes   2 No

    Explain:

28. Are you tenured?

    1 Yes   2 No

29. Do you see a difference between the types of students who take your course on the psychology of women and those who take other courses in your department?

    1 Yes   2 No

    Explain:

30. This is your space! Please comment on any of the items in this survey. Also mention additional issues you believe are important in teaching the psychology of women course.

Part 1

General Resources

1

General Resources for Teaching the Psychology of Women

Sample Textbooks on the Psychology of Women

Bardwick, J. (1970). *Feminine Personality and Conflict.* Belmont, Calif.: Brooks/Cole.

Bardwick, J. (1971). *Psychology of Women: A Study of Biocultural Conflicts.* New York: Harper & Row.

Bardwick, J. (Ed.) (1972). *Readings on the Psychology of Women.* New York: Harper & Row.

Basow, S. (1986). *Gender Stereotypes: Traditions and Alternatives.* Monterey, Calif.: Brooks/Cole.

Cox, S. (Ed.) (1976). *Female Psychology: The Emerging Self.* Chicago: Science Research Associates.

Cox, S. (Ed.) (1981). *Female Psychology: The Emerging Self.* New York: St. Martin's Press.

Deaux, K. (1976). *The Behavior of Women and Men.* Monterey, Calif.: Brooks/Cole.

Donelson, E., and Gullahorn, J. (1977). *Women: A Psychological Perspective.* New York: Wiley.

Doyle, J.A. (1985). *Sex and Gender: The Human Experience.* Dubuque, IA.: William C. Brown.

Freeman, J. (Ed.) (1975). *Women: A Feminist Perspective.* Palo Alto, Calif.: Mayfield.

Frieze, I., Parsons, J., Johnson, P., Ruble, D., and Zellman, G. (1978). *Women and Sex Roles: A Social Psychological Perspective.* New York: Norton.

Gullahorn, J.E. (1979). *Psychology and Women: In Transition.* Washington, DC: C.H. Winsont and Sons.

Hyde, J.S. (1985). *Half the Human Experience.* Lexington, Mass.: D.C. Heath.

Hyde, J.S., and Rosenberg, B.G. (1980). *Half the Human Experience: The Psychology of Women.* Lexington, Mass.: D.C. Heath.

Kaplan, A.G., and Bean, J.P. (1976). *Beyond Sex Role Stereotypes: Readings Toward a Psychology of Androgyny.* Boston: Little Brown.

Lott, B. (1987). *Women's lives: Themes and Variations in Gender Learning.* Monterey, Calif.: Brooks/Cole.

Matlin, M. W. (1987). *The Psychology of Women.* New York: Holt, Rinehart, Winston.

Miller, J.B. (1976). *Toward a New Psychology of Women.* Boston: Beacon Press.

O'Leary, V.E. (1977). *Toward Understanding Women.* Monterey, Calif.: Brooks/Cole.

O'Leary, V.E., Wallston, B.S., and Unger, R.K. (1985). *Women, Gender, and Social Psychology.* Hillsdale, NJ: Erlbaum.

Sherman, J. (1971). *On the Psychology of Women: A Survey of Empirical Studies.* Springfield, IL: Charles C. Thomas.

Sherman, M.A., and Denmark, F.L. (Eds.) (1978). *The Psychology of Women: Future Directions in Research.* New York: Psychological Dimensions.

Tavris, C. (Ed.) (1973). *The Female Experience.* Del Mar, Calif.: Communications Research Machines.

Tavris, C., and Wade, C. (1984). *The Longest War: Sex Differences in Perspective.* New York: Harcourt Brace Jovanovich.

Walsh, M.R. (Ed.) *The Psychology of Women: Ongoing Debates.* New Haven: Yale University Press.

Williams, J.H. (1987). *Psychology of Women: Behavior in a Biosocial Context.* New York: Norton.

Williams, J.H. (Ed.) (1979). *Psychology of Women: Selected Readings.* New York: Norton.

Teaching the Psychology of women: Sample references and conference presentations.

Billingham, K.A. (1982). "Building a course on psychology of women: Method and resources." *Psychology of Women Quarterly, 7,* 32–44.

Brown, A., Goodwin, B.J., Hall, B.A., and Jackson-Lowman, H. (1985). A review of psychology of women textbooks: Focus on the Afro-American women." *Psychology of Women Quarterly, 9,* 29–38.

Bunch, C., and Pollack, S. (Eds.) (1983). *Learning Our Way: Essays in Feminist Education.* Trumansburg, NY: The Crossing Press.

Carmen, E., and Driver, F. (1982). "Teaching women's studies: Values in conflict." *Psychology of Women Quarterly, 7,* 81–95.

Clarey, J., Hutchins, J., Powers, V., and Thiem, L. (1985). "Feminist education: Transforming the research seminar." *Journal of Thought, 20,* 147–161.

Collins, P.H. (1986). "The emerging theory and pedagogy of Black women's studies." *Feminist Issues, 6,* 3–18.

Conway, J. (1974). "Coeducation and women's studies: Two approaches to the question of women's place in the contemporary university." *Daedalus, 103,* 239–249.

Culley, M., and Portuges, C. (Eds.). (1985). *Gendered Subjects: The Dynamics of Feminist Teaching.* Boston: Routledge & Kegan Paul.

Davis, B.H. (1983). "Teaching the feminist minority." In C. Bunch and S. Pollack (Eds.). *Learning Our Way: Essays in Feminist Education.* Trumansburg, NY: The Crossing Press.

Freedman, R.J., Golub, S., and Krauss, B. (1982). "Mainstreaming the psychology of women into the core curriculum." *Teaching of Psychology, 9,* 165–168.

Golub, S., Freedman, R.J., Krauss, B., Carpenter, R., Quinta, K., and Russo, N. (1984). "Resources for introductory psychology of women content and methodology into the psychology core curriculum." *Psychological Document, 14,* 1,1.

Golub, S. and Freedman, R.J. (Eds.). (1987). *Psychology of Women: Resources for a Core Curriculum.* New York: Garland.

Johnson, M. (1982). "Research on teaching the psychology of women." *Psychology of Women Quarterly, 7,* 96–104.

Kahn, A.S., and Jean, P.J. (1983). "Integration and elimination or separation and redefinition: The future of the psychology of women." *Signs, 8,* 659–671.

Lord, S.B. (1982). "Teaching the psychology of women: Examination of a teaching-learning model." *Psychology of Women Quarterly, 7,* 71–80.

Maher, F. (1985). "Pedagogies for the gender-balanced classroom." *Journal of Thought, 20,* 48–64.

Paludi, M.A. (1986). "Teaching the psychology of gender roles: Some life-stage considerations." *Teaching of Psychology, 13,* 133–138.

Richardson, M.S. (1982). "Sources of tension in teaching the psychology of women." *Psychology of Women Quarterly, 7,* 45–54.

Riger, S. (1978). "A technique for teaching the psychology of women: Content analysis." *Teaching of Psychology, 5*, 221–223.

Riger, S. (1979). "On teaching the psychology of women. *Teaching of Psychology, 6*, 113–114.

Russo, N.F. (1982). "Psychology of women: Analysis of the faculty and courses of an emerging field." *Psychology of Women Quarterly, 7*, 18–31.

Sholley, R.K. (1986). "Value of book discussions in a psychology of women course." *Teaching of Psychology, 13*, 151–153.

Unger, R.K. (1982). "Advocacy versus scholarship revisited: Issues in the psychology of women." *Psychology of Women Quarterly, 7*, 5–17.

Vedouato, S., and Vaughter, R. (1980). "Psychology of women courses changing sexist and sex-typed attitudes." *Psychology of Women Quarterly, 4*, 587–590.

Walsh, M.R. (1985). "The psychology of women course: A continuing catalyst for change." *Teaching of Psychology, 12*, 198–202.

Westkott, M. (1979). "Feminist criticism of the social sciences." *Harvard Educational Review, 49*, 422–430.

Sample Conference Presentations on Teaching the Psychology of Women

American Psychological Association, 1985

> Conversation Hour: Developing networks for faculty teaching a psychology of women course
> Chairperson: Mary Roth Walsh (University of Lowell)
> Panel: Jacquelynne Eccles (University of Michigan
>   Irene Hanson Frieze (University of Pittsburgh)
>   Linda Ruprecht (New Mexico State University
>   Barbara Sholley (University of Richmond)

Association for Women in Psychology, 1986

> Conversation Hour: The psychology of women course as a catalyst for change
> Chairperson: Mary Roth Walsh (University of Lowell)
> Panel: Kathryn Quina (University of Rhode Island)
>   Michele Paludi (Kent State University)
>   Alice Ray Brown-Collins (Brown University)
>   Chalsa Loo (University of California, Los Angeles)
>   Ellyn Kaschak (San Jose State University)

American Psychological Association, 1986

Conversation Hour: Surviving as a feminist researcher and teacher
Chairperson: Michele A. Paludi (Kent State University)
Panel: Virginia O'Leary (O'Leary and Associates)
  Sue Rosenberg Zalk (Hunter College)
  Irene Hanson Frieze (University of Pittsburgh)
  Janet Shibley Hyde (University of Wisconsin, Madison)
  Sandra Shullman (Organizational Horizons, Inc.)
  Nancy Benham (Kent State University)
  Vivian Makosky (American Psychological Association)
  Leonore Tiefer (Beth Israel Hospital)

American Educational Research Association: Special Interest Group: Research on Women and Education, 1985

Conversation Hour: Teaching the new psychology of women
Chairperson: Mary Roth Walsh (University of Lowell)
Panel: Patricia Arrendondo (Boston University)
  Deborah Belle (Boston University)
  Alice Ray Brown-Collins (Brown University)
  Michele Paludi (Kent State University)
  Kathryn Quina (University of Rhode Island)
  Barbara Sholley (University of Richmond)

American Psychological Association, 1986

Discussion Session: Using knowledge as an empowerment strategy:
  Psychology of women
Chairperson: Mary Roth Walsh (University of Lowell
Panel Judith Alpert (New York University)
  Elaine Carmen (University of North Carolina, Chapel Hill)
  Paula Caplan (Ontario Institute for Studies in Education)
  Margaret Matlin (State University of New York, Geneseo)
  Patricia Rieker (Dana Farber Cancer Institute)
  Barbara Sholley (University of Richmond)
  Carol Whitehill (Kresge College)
  Althea Smith (Boston College)

Association for Women in Psychology, 1986

Conversation Hour: Surviving as a feminist researcher
Chairperson: Michele Paludi (Kent State University)
Panel: Louise Fitzgerald (University of California, Santa Barbara)
  Nancy Henley (University of California, Los Angeles)
  Alice Collins (Brown University

Mary Roth Walsh (University of Lowell)
Virginia O'Leary (O'Leary and Associates)
Patricia Rozee-Koker (Indiana State University)
Barbara Gutek (Claremont Graduate School)

American Educational Research Association, 1987

Invited Discussion: Surviving as a feminist scholar
Chairperson: Michele Paludi (Kent State University)
Panel: Sandy Shullman (Organizational Horizons, Inc.)
   Nancy Benham (Kent State University)
   Mary Koss (Kent State University)
   Vivian Makosky (American Psychological Association)
   Marilee Niehoff (University of Texas, Arlington)
   Carole Garrison (University of Akron)

American Psychological Association, 1987

Preconvention Workshop: Teaching the psychology of women
Chairperson: Mary Roth Walsh (University of Lowell)
Panel: Margaret Matlin (State University of New York, Geneseo)
   Juanita Williams (University of South Florida)
   Bernice Lott (University of Rhode Island)

Midwestern Society for Feminist Studies, 1987

Discussion Session: Teaching feminism in the classroom: Networking
   among educators
Chairperson: Michele A. Paludi (Hunter College)
Panel: Kathryn Quina (University of Rhode Island)
   Karen Maitland Schilling (Miami University)
   Susan Basow (Lafayette College)
   Michael Stevenson (Ball State University)
   Joan Tronto (Hunter College)
   Carole Corcoran (Mary Washington College)
   Susan Hardin (University of Akron)
   Linda Subich (University of Akron)

Association for Women in Psychology, 1988

Preconference Workshop: Integrating the scholarship on women of Color
   and ethnicity into the psychology of women
   course
Chairpersons: Michele Paludi and Darlene DeFour (Hunter College)

American Psychological Association, 1989

Roundtable Discussion: New Wave of Conservative Politics or Second Stage
of Feminism?
Chairperson: Michele Paludi (Hunter College)
Participants: Pat Rozee-Koker (California State, Long Beach)
Mary Kite (Ball State University)
Margaret Matlin (State University of New York, Geneseo)
Bea Krauss (College of New Rochelle)

American Psychological Association, 1989

Preconvention Workshop: Teaching the psychology of women
Chairperson: Mary Roth Walsh (University of Lowell)
Participants: Margaret Matlin (State University of New York, Geneseo)
Janet Shibley Hyde (University of Wisconsin, Madison)

Handbooks, Anthologies, Bibliographies

Baer, N., & Sherif, C. (1974). *Topical Bibliography on the Psychology of
Women.* Washington, DC: American Psychological Association.

Ballou, P.K. (1980). *Women: A Bibliography of Bibliographies.* Boston, Mass.:
G.K. Hall and Co.

Beere, C.A. (1979). *Women and Women's Issues: A Handbook of Tests and
Measures.* San Francisco, Calif.: Jossey-Bass.

Boston Lesbian Psychologies Collective (Eds.) (1987). *Lesbian Psychologies:
Explorations and Challenges.* Champaign, IL: University of Illinois
Press.

Bronstein, P., and Quina, K. (Eds.). (1988). *Toward a Psychology of People:
Resources for Gender and Sociocultural Awareness.* Washington, DC:
American Psychological Association.

Cardinale, S. (1982). *Anthologies by and about Women: An Analytical Index.*
Westport, Conn.: Greenwood.

Dilling, C., and Claster, B.L. (Eds.). (1986). *Female Psychology: A Partially
Annotated Bibliography.* New York: New York City Coalition for Women's
Health.

Feminist Periodicals: A Current Listing of Contents. Madison, WI: Office of the
women's studies librarian at large, University of Wisconsin System
1981–present.

Stineman, E. (1979). *Women's studies: A Recommended Core Bibliography.*
Littleton, Co.: Libraries Unlimited, Inc.

31

Walstedt, J.J. (1973). *Psychology of Women: A Partially Annotated Bibliography.* KNOW.

Wheeler, H.R. (1975). *Womanhood Media Supplement: Additional Current Resources about Women.* Metuchen, NJ: The Scarecrow Press.

Library Resources in the Psychology of Women

For valuable discussions on how to use the card catalog and finding books on women's issues, consult:

Searing, S.E. (1985). *Introduction to Library Research in Women's Studies.* Boulder: Westview Press.

Lynn, N.B., Matasar, A.B., and Rosenberg, M.B. (1974). *Research Guide in Women's Studies.* Morristown, NJ: General Learning Press.

In addition:

Women's Studies Abstracts: This is a basic indexing and abstracting source for research on the study of women. It covers not only feminist and women's studies sources, but selectively covers articles of 1,000 words or more in journals in many other fields. It began publication in 1972 and is published quarterly. It is available in printed format only.

Studies on Women Abstracts: This index has been published bimonthly since 1985. It is international in scope, scanning major journals and books. It includes journal articles, books and book chapters. It, too, is available in printed format only.

Catalyst Resource on the Workforce and Women: This database, available online only, is produced by the Catalyst Information Center (250 Park Avenue, New York City). It covers many aspects of women's issues, focusing on those which relate to career and work areas. There is no printed index, but accessions lists are published and the collection is open to the public by appointment.

In addition to these three specialized sources, the following databases all provide useful information:

ERIC (Educational Resources Information Center); The online version covers the years 1966 on. It is available in printed form as *Current Index to Journals in Education* (1969-) which indexes articles from over 700 major education and education related journals, and *Resources in Education* (1966-), which indexes education related documents.

Sociological Abstracts: Available online (1963-) and in printed format (1952-). This index scans over 1200 journals and other serial publications to cover the world's literature in sociology and related areas in social and behavioral sciences.

Psychological Abstracts: Available online as PsychInfo (1967-) and in printed form (1927-). This is an international service which covers over 1300 journals and other publications in psychology and behavioral sciences.

ABI/INFORM: Available online (1971-). Almost 700 publications in business and related fields are scanned. The database contains much useful information on women, focusing on career and workforce issues. A somewhat comparable printed resource is *Business Periodicals Index* (1958-) which is itself available online and covers approximately 300 sources.

Legal Resources Index: Available online (1980-). The database covers over 750 key law journals and six law newspapers, plus legal monographs. It provides a legal perspective on women's issues. A useful printed index is the *Index to Legal Periodicals* (1908-), which is also available online.

Index of Economic Articles: Available online as *Economic Literature Index* (19690) and in printed form (1886-). This covers approximately 260 economic journals and 200 monographs. It is valuable for the economic perspective it provides on women's issues.

For more general, less scholarly material there is:

National Newspaper Index: Available online and in microfiche (1979-) which covers the New York Times, Christian Science Monitor, Wall Street Journal, Washington Post, and Los Angeles Times.

Magazine Index: Available online and in microfiche (1959-) which indexes more than 430 popular magazines. Comparable printed resources are *Reader's Guide to Periodical Literature* (1900-) which indexes about 200 general interest magazines, and *Access* (1975-) which indexes national general interest publications not covered in Reader's Guide.

Alternative Press Index: Available in printed format only (1969-). This index covers close to 200 leftist and radical opinion journals and newspapers from the English speaking world.

A useful and interesting resource is the *Social Sciences Citation Index* (1971-), available online as *Social SciSearch* (1972-). In addition to conventional research by title words, author, journal names, it is possible to search an author's cited references in this source. Beginning with a single useful source article, one can trace other authors who are citing that source and who presumably are researching the same or related areas.

Female Studies I–V
  Available from KNOW, Inc.
  Box 86031
  Pittsburgh, PA 15221

The new guide to current female studies
  KNOW, Inc.
  Box 86031
  Pittsburgh, PA 15221

Women's Studies: A program for colleges and universities
  Dr. Elizabeth Farians
  6125 Webbland Place
  Cincinnati, OH 45213

Resources for Women's Studies

Monographs distributed by the National Institute of Education (U.S. Department of Health, Education, and Welfare, Washington, DC 20208).

The effectiveness of women's studies teaching

Women's studies as a catalyst for faculty development

The impact of women's studies on the campus and the disciplines

The involvement of minority women in women's studies

Women's studies in the community college

Re-entry women involved in women's studies

The relationship between women's studies, career development, and vocational choice

Women's studies graduates

Publishing Houses, Clearinghouses, and Libraries

The Feminist Press
  City University of New York
  311 East 94 Street
  New York, NY 10128

KNOW, Inc.
  P.O. Box 86031
  Pittsburgh, PA 15221

Women's History Research Center
  2325 Oak Street
  Berkeley, CA 94708

Schlesinger Library
  Radcliffe College
  Cambridge, MA 02138

Sophia Smith Collection
  Smith College Library
  Northhampton, MA 01063

National Women's History Project
  P.O. Box 3716
  Santa Rosa, CA 95402

Clearinghouse on Women's Issues
  Dupont Circle Building
  Suite 924
  1346 Connecticut Avenue, N.W.
  Washington, DC 20036

Organizations Concerned with Women's Issues

This is a compilation of several national and regional organizations concerned with issues devoted to women's concerns in the academe. Also included are associations providing resources on women's issues, such as government agencies, research institutes, journals, publishers, and clearinghouses. This coverage is not comprehensive. Additional listings are presented within each of the chapters in this manual. Further information may be obtained from "A Woman's Yellow Pages," published by the Federation of Organizations for Professional Women, 1825 Connecticut Avenue, NW, Suite 403, Washington, DC, 20009.

Resources

National Women's Studies Association
  University of Maryland
  203 Behavioral and Social Sciences Building
  College Park, MD 20742

National Organization for Women
  425 13th Street, NW
  Suite 723
  Washington, DC 20004

National Institute for Women of Color
  1712 N. St. NW
  Washington, DC 20036

National Network of Minority Women in Science
Association for the Advancement of Science
1776 Massachusetts Avenue, NW
Washington, DC 20036

Asian Women United
170 Park Row # 5A
New York, NY 10038

Center for Mexican American Studies
The University of Texas
Austin, TX 78712

Women's Bureau
U.S. Department of Labor
Washington, DC 20210

Federation of Organizations for Professional Women
1825 Connecticut Ave., NW
Washington, DC 20009

Project on the Status and Education of Women
1818 R St. NW
Washington, DC 20009

Mid-Atlantic Center for Race Equity
The American University
4900 Massachusetts Ave., NW
Washington, DC 20036

American Indian Women's Service League
617 Second Avenue
Seattle, Washington 98104

Association of Black Women in Higher Education
30 Limerick Drive
Albany, NY 12204

Women's Educational Equity Act Program
Education Development Center
55 Chapel Street
Newton, MA 02160

Women's Studies Newsletter
  National Women's Studies Association
  4102 Foreign Languages Building
  University of Maryland
  College Park, MD 20742

Adult Educational Association of the USA
  810 18 Street NW
  Washington, DC 20036

American Association for the Advancement of Science
  Women's Caucus
  1776 Massachusetts Avenue, NW
  Washington, DC 20036

American Association for Affirmative Action
  Institute of Urban Affairs and Research
  Howard University
  2900 Van Ness Street NW
  Washington, DC 20008

Midwestern Society for Feminist Studies
  Michael Stevenson
  Women's and Gender Studies
  Ball State University
  Muncie, IN 47306

Association for Women in Psychology
  Jan Fontaine
  Education Department
  Indiana University of Pennsylvania
  Indiana, PA 15705

American Association of Community and Junior Colleges
  Center for Women's Opportunities
  One Dupont Circle, NW
  Suite 140
  Washington, DC 20036

American Educational Research Association
  Special Interest Group: Research on Women and Education
  1230 17 Street, NW
  Washington, DC 20036

American Psychological Association
  Women's Programs Office
  1200 17 Street, NW
  Washington, DC 2036

Center for the Study, Education, and Advancement of Women
University of California, Berkeley
Building T-9, Room 112
Berkeley, CA 94720

Centers for Research on Women (University Affiliated)

A complete list of centers for research on women has been compiled by the National Council for Research on Women. For more information contact the National Council for Research on Women, 47–49 East 65th St., New York, NY 10021. The *Women's Studies Quarterly* (Feminist Press) prints a list describing women's research centers each spring. The Women's Research and Education Institute publishes *A Directory of Selected Women's Research and Policy Centers.* This is available from WREI, 294 Fourth St., SE, Washington, DC 20003.

Name	University	Address
Southwest Institute for Research on Women	University of Arizona	Modern Languages 269 Tucson, AZ 85721
Pembroke Center for Teaching and Research on Women	Brown University	Box 1958 Providence, RI 02912
Center for the Study, Education, and Advancement of Women	University of California, Berkeley	Room 112 Building T-9 Berkeley, CA 94720
Women's Resources and Research Center	University of California, Davis	10 Lower Freeborn Hall Davis, CA 95616
Center for the Study of Women	University of California, Los Angeles	236 A Kinsey Hall Los Angeles, CA 90064
Higher Education Research Institute	University of California, Los Angeles	Grad. School of Educ. 405 Hilgard Ave. Los Angeles, CA 90024
Center for Women's Studies Research and Resources Institute	University of Cincinnati	Room 150 McMicken Hall Mail Location 164 Cincinnati, OH 45221
Center for the Study of Women and Society	CUNY Graduate School and University Center	33 West 42nd St. New York, NY 10036
Institute for Women and Work	Cornell University	New York State School of Industrial and Labor Relations 15 East 26th St. New York, NY 10010
Women's Studies Research Center	Duke University - University of N. Carolina	119 East Duke Building Durham, NC 27708

The Women's Studies Program and Policy Center	George Washington University	Stuart Hall Room 203 Washington, DC 20052
Higher Education Resource Services, New England	Wellesley College	Cheever House Wellesley, MA 02181
Higher Education Resource Services, Mid-America	Colorado Women's College Campus, University of Denver	Denver, CO 80220
Higher Education Resource Services, West	University of Utah	Women's Resource Center 293 Olpin Union Salt Lake City, UT 84112
Center for Research on Women	Memphis State University	College of Arts & Sciences Memphis, TN 38152
Center for Continuing Education of Women	University of Michigan	350 South Thayer St. Ann Arbor, MI 48109
Center for Advanced Feminist Studies	University of Minnesota	492 Ford Hall 224 Church St. SE Minneapolis, MN 55455
Center for Women in Government	State University of New York at Albany	Draper Hall Room 302 1400 Washington Ave. Albany, NY 12222
Center for the Study of Women in Society	University of Oregon	Room 636 Prince Lucien Campbell Hall College of Arts & Sciences Eugene, OR 97403
Center for Rural Women	Pennsylvania State University	College of Agriculture 201 Agricultural Admin. Bldg. University Park, PA 16802
Alice Paul Center for the Study of Women	University of Pennsylvania	106 Logan Hall, CN Philadelphia, PA 19104
Mary Ingraham Bunting Institute	Radcliffe College	10 Garden St. Cambridge, MA 02138
The Henry Murray Research Center	Radcliffe College	77 Brattle St. Cambridge, MA 02138
The Arthur and Elizabeth Schlesinger Library	Radcliffe College	10 Garden St. Cambridge, MA 02138
Center for the American Woman and Politics	Rutgers University	Eagleton Institute of Politics New Brunswick, NJ 08903

Institute for Research on Women	Rutgers University	Douglass College New Brunswick, NJ 08903
Project on Women and Social Change	Smith College	138 Elm St. Northamton, MA 01063
Program for the Study of Women and Men in Society	University of Southern California	Taper Hall 331M Los Angeles, CA 90089
Women's Resource and Research Center	Spelman College	Box 362 Atlanta, CA 30314
Center for Research on Women	Stanford University	Serra House, Serra St. Stanford, CA 94305
Northwest Center for Research on Women	University of Washington	Cunningham Hall AJ-50 Seattle, WA 98195
Center for Research on Women	Wellesley College	828 Washington St. Wellesley, MA 02181
Women's Studies Program and Research Center	University of Wisconsin, Madison	209 North Brooks St. Madison, WI 53715

Centers for Research on Women (Non-University Affiliated)

Center	*Address*
American Council on Education	One Dupont Circle, NW Washington, DC 20036
Association of American Colleges Project on the Status and Education of Women	1818 R Street, NW Washington, DC 20009
Business and Professional Women's Foundation	2012 Massachusetts Ave., NW Washington, DC 20036
Center for Women Policy Studies	2000 P Street, NW Suite 508 Washington, DC 20036
Equity Policy Center	4818 Drummond Avenue Chevy Chase, MD 20815
The Institute for Research in History	1133 Broadway Suite 923 New York, NY 10010
International Center for Research on Women	1717 Massachusetts Ave., NW Suite 501 Washington, DC 20036

National Association for Women Deans, Administrators, and Counselors	1325 18th St., NW Suite 210 Washington, DC 20036
Project on Equal Education Rights	1413 K Street, NW 9th Floor Washington, DC 20005
Program of Policy Research on Women and Families Urban Institute	2100 M St., NW Washington, DC 20037
Women's Interart Center	549 W. 52nd St. New York, NY 10019
The Women's Research and Education Institute, Congressional Caucus for Women's Issues	204 Fourth St., SE Washington, DC 20003

Sample References on the History of Women in Psychology

Benjamin, L.T. Jr. (1980). Women in psychology: Biography and autobiography. *Psychology of Women Quarterly, 5*, 140–144.

Bernstein, M.D., and Russo, N.F. (1974). "The history of psychology revisited: Or, up with our foremothers." *American Psychologist, 29*, 130–134.

Bryan, A.I., and Boring, E.G. (1946). "Women in American psychology: Statistics from the OPP questionnaire." *American Psychologist, 1*, 71–79.

Bryan, A.I., and Boring, E.G. (1947). "Women in American psychology: Factors affecting their professional careers." *American Psychologist, 2*, 3–20/

Denmark, F.L. (1977). "The psychology of women: An overview of an emerging field." *Personality and Social Psychology Bulletin, 3*, 356–367.

Denmark, F.L. (1979). "Women in psychology in the United States." In A.M. Briscoe and S.M. Pfafflin (Eds.) *Expanding the Role of Women in the Sciences.* Annals of the New York Academy of Sciences, *323*, 1057–1065.

Flexner, E. (1973). *Mary Wollstonecraft.* Baltimore: Penguin.

Furumoto, L. (1979). Mary Whiton Calkins (1863–1930): "Fourteenth president of the American Psychological Association." *Journal of the History of the Behavioral Sciences, 15*, 346–356.

Furumoto, L. (1980). "Mary Whiton Calkins (1863–1930). *Psychology of Women Quarterly, 5*, 55–67.

Furumoto, L., and Scarborough, E. (1986). "Placing women in the history of psychology: The first American women psychologist." *American Psychologist, 41*, 35–42.

Gavin, E. (1986, August). "Who's who among women in psychology." Paper presented at the American Psychological Association, Washington, DC.

Goodman, E.S. (1980). "Margaret F. Washburn (1871–1939): "First women Ph.D. in psychology." *Psychology of Women Quarterly, 5,* 69–80.

Goodman, E.S. (1983). "History's choices." *Contemporary Psychology, 28,* 667–669.

Levin, M. (Ed.) (1984). *In the Shadow of the Past: Psychology Portrays the Sexes: A Social and Intellectual History.* New York: Columbia University Press.

Mednick, M. (1978). "Psychology of women: Research issues and trends." *New York Academy of Sciences Annals, 309,* 77–92.

O'Connell, A., Anderson, N., Astin, H., Mednick, M., and Russo, N. (1986, August). "Eminent women in psychology: Personal and historical perspectives." Symposium presented at the American Psychological Association, Washington, DC.

O'Connell, A., and Russo, N. (Eds.) (1983). *Models of Achievement: Reflections of Eminent Women in Psychology.* New York: Columbia University Press.

Russo, N.F. and Denmark, F.L. (1987). "Contributions of women to psychology." *Annual Review of Psychology, 38,* 279–298.

Scarborough, E. and Furumoto, L. (1987). *Untold lives: The first Generation of American Women Psychologists.* New York: Columbia University Press.

Shields, S. (1975). "Functionalism, Darwinism, and the psychology of women: A study in social myth." *American Psychologist, 10,* 739–754.

Shields, S. (1975). "Ms. Pilgrim's progress: The contribution of Leta Stetter Hollingworth to the psychology of women." *American Psychologist, 30,* 852–857.

Sexton, V. (1974). "Women in American psychology: An overview." *Journal of International Understanding, 9,* 66–77.

Stevens, G., and Gardner, S. (1982). *The Women of Psychology: Pioneers and Innovators.* Cambridge, MA: Schenkman.

Stevens, G., and Gardner, S. (1982). *The Women of Psychology: Expansion and Refinement.*

Viney, W., and Zorich, S. (1982). "Contributions to the history of psychology: Dorothea Dix and the history of psychology." *Psychological Reports, 50,* 212–218.

Organizations Dealing with the History of Women in Psychology

Chciron: The International Society for the History of Behavioral and Social Sciences

Dr. R. Evans
Yale Gordon College of Liberal Arts
University of Baltimore
1420 N. Charles St.
Baltimore, MD 21201–5779

Division 26 of the American Psychological Association, History of Psychology

American Psychological Association
1200 17th St. NW
Washington, DC 20036

History of Science Society

Publication Office
215 South 34th St.
Philadelphia, PA 19104-6310

Forum for History of Human Science

Laurel Furumoto
Psychology
Wellesley College
Wellesley, MA 02181

Sample Listing of Filmmakers/Distributors

Additional names and addresses may be found in each of the subsequent chapters.

New Day Films
114 Park St.
Brookline, MA 02146

Filmakers Library
124 E. 40th St.
Suite 901
New York, NY 10016

Churchill Films
662 N. Robertson Blvd.
Los Angeles, CA 90069

Cinema Guild
1697 Broadway
New York, NY 10019

Women Make Movies
225 Lafayette St.
New York, NY 10012

Iris Films
Box 5353
Berkeley, Calif. 94703

Educational Media
P.O. Box 1991
University, Alabama 35486

Ishtar Films
P.O. Box 51
Patterson, NY 12563

The Film Distribution Center
1028 Industry Drive
Seattle, WA 98188

Harrison, Kooden, and Associates
123 W. 44th St.
New York, NY 10036

Cambridge Documentary Films
P.O. Box 385
Cambridge, MA 02139

Sample Listing of Publishers of Books on Women's Lives and Experiences

Publishers	Address
Kelsey St. Press	P.O. Box 9235 Berkeley, CA 94705
Listen Real Loud: News of Women's Liberation Worldwide	1501 Cherry St. Philadelphia, PA 19102
Ladyslipper	P.O. Box 3124 Durham, NC 27705
Lesbian Contradiction: A Journal of Irreverent Feminism	10007 N. 47th St. Seattle, WA 98103
Margaretdaughters Inc.	Central Park Station P.O. Box 907 Buffalo, NY 14215

National Women's Health Network	224 7th St. SE Washington, DC 20003
New Women's Press Ltd.	P.O. Box 47-339 Aukland, New Zealand
Southern Feminist	P.O. Box 1846 Athens, GA 30603
Pandora Book Peddlers	68 W. Palisade Ave. Englewood, NJ 07631
Onlywoman Press	38 Mount Pleasant London WCIZ OAP
Sage Women's Educational Press, Inc.	Box 42741 Atlanta, GA 30311
The Crossing Press	P.O. Box 1048 22-D Roache Road Freedom, CA 95019
The Feminist Press	311 E. 94th St. New York, NY 10128
The Seal Press	3131 Western Ave. Suite 410 Seattle, WA 92121
Through the Looking Glass	P.O. Box 22061 Seattle, WA 98122
Williams-Wallace Publishers Tiger Lily Magazine-Women of Color	2 Silver Avenue Toronto, CANADA M6R 3A2

Sample Syllabi From Courses on the Psychology of Women

I appreciate the contributions of course syllabi from the following individuals:

Carole Corcoran, Mary Washington College

Michael Stevenson, Ball State University

Ellen Kimmel, University of South Florida

These instructors of courses in women's issues may be contacted about their materials. Additional information about instructors of psychology of women courses may be obtained from:

Women's Program Office
American Psychological Association
1200 17th St. NW
Washington, DC 20036

Syllabus I: Carole Corcoran

Mary Washington College

Texts:

Women/A Feminist Perspective, *edited by J. Freeman, 1984, 3rd edition.*
Psychology of Women/Selected Readings, *edited by J. Williams, 1985, 2nd edition.*

Guidelines/activities for learning objectives/course evaluation contract

1. Course Participation
   attendance, class participation, discussion leader, presentation activities, assignments

2. Course Readings
   assigned text readings, additional readings

3. Written Work
   keeping a journal, interviews, reaction papers, book/journal article reviews, media portfolio

4. Independent Pursuits
   semester project and presentation

Grading guidelines

A Work outstanding in quality. Unusual mastery of assigned work, but also has independently sought out additional materials. Demonstrate ability to discover new insights and relate to work at hand.

B Work higher in quality, more than satisfactory. Ability and initiative to fulfill more than basic requirement of the course.

C Work fulfills basic requirements of course (participation, readings, written assignments, project).

D Below basic requirements in either quality or quantity.

F Unsatisfactory in either quality or quantity.

Assumption 1: The course should be a laboratory of feminist principles.

Assumption 2: The traditional patriarchal teaching-learning model is dysfunctional in the development of healthy women (and men).

Assumption 3: Every individual in the class is a potential teaching resource.

Assumption 4: Integration is imperative for the development of healthy, whole women (and men).

Assumption 5: Effective human behavior in social interactions and within social systems is related to understanding the relationship between the personal and the political.Assumption 6: A psychology of women course should (a) deal with the female of the species only, and (b) treat the female as a normal human model.

Assumption 7:The subjective, personal experience of women (and men) is valid and important.

Assumption 8: The students should ultimately assume responsibility for her own learning and growth.

Assumption 9: Cooperation among students in pursuing learning objectives creates a more positive learning climate than does competition.

Assumption 10: Providing vehicles outside of class through which students can deal with personal feelings and frustrations (*e.g.*, journals, discussion groups) enhances the quality of classroom discussion.

Assumption 11: The generic use of terms such as woman and the female pronoun to refer to humans is an effective teaching/learning tool.

Assumption 12: Both women and men should be exposed to and have an understanding of the developmental and social psychology of women. However, a structure should be provided which allows women to meet with women and men with men for a portion of the time.

(Based on Lord, 1982)

Self-Evaluation Form
Date _____

Topic _____

A. Readings

I did ____/did not ____/other ____ (explain below)/complete assigned readings prior to the class discussion.

List any additional readings you completed that are relevant to this topic:

Comments/Explanation:

B. Participation

I did ____/did not ____/participate in the class discussion.

On the scale below, circle the number which you think describes the extent of your personal contribution to the discussion.

not at all   1   2   3   4   5   6   7   to a great degree

C. Effectiveness

Name _____   Rating _____

Name _____   Rating _____

To what extent do you think this person was well-informed and effective as a discussion leader? Choose a number from the scale below and write it in the blank next to the person's name.

not at all   1   2   3   4   5   6   7   to a great degree

Please give the discussion leader(s) feedback on her (their) particular strengths and/or weaknesses. Include any other comments that you feel would be helpful. (Your comments will be shared with discussion leaders but you will not be identified by name.)

D. Pledge and Name

Midterm Evaluation Form

For each class meeting and where appropriate you should indicate whether you attended class (AT), whether you completed the required readings (RR), whether you completed additional readings (AR)—remember, you should be keeping a bibliography of these, whether you wrote on the topic (WR), and whether you participated in the discussion (DS). Other questions that you should consider in completing your evaluation form are as follows: Did you integrate required readings and additional readings into your writing? Did you maintain a balance between personal experiences and scholarly material in your writing? Have you made significant progress on your contract and learning objectives?

Language	AT: _____
	RR: _____ Steinem
	_____ Richardson
	_____ APA Guidelines
	AR: _____
	WR: _____
	DS: _____
? Panel	AT: _____
	AR: _____
	WR: _____
	DS: _____
History	AT: _____
	RR: _____ Shields
	_____ Rosenberg
	AR: _____
	WR: _____
	DS: _____
Bryn Mawr Film	AT: _____
	AR: _____
	WR: _____
Differences	AT: _____
	RR: _____ Unger
	_____ Deaux
	_____ Fausto-Sterling
	AR: _____
	WR: _____
	DS: _____
Domestic Violence	AT: _____
	AR: _____
	WR: _____
	DS: _____
Socialization	AT: _____
	RR: _____ Weitzman
	AR: _____

	WR:	
	DS:	
After the Revolution	AT:	
	AR:	
	WR:	
Menses Menopause	AT:	
	RR:	Golub
		Fausto-Sterling
		Steinem
	AR:	
	WR:	
	DS:	
Myth or Reality	AT:	
	AR:	
	WR:	
Rape	AT:	
	RR:	Herman
		Leidig
		Sheffield
	AR:	
	WR:	
	DS:	
Freud & Feminism	AT:	
	AR:	
	WR:	
	DS:	
Body Image	AT:	
	AR:	
	WR:	
	DS:	

Midterm Progress:

Give yourself an estimated overall grade_____.

(Please choose one letter grade, feel free to use plus or minus.)

Give yourself an estimated midterm grade reflecting your progress on the following:

Project _____.

Writing _____.

Class Discussion _____.

Discussion Leader (if applicable) _____.

Comments:

Name and Pledge:

Syllabus II: Michael Stevenson

Ball State University

The course provides students with the opportunity to critically appraise empirical research and theory on the psychological functioning of women. The course emphasizes topics that have been approached scientifically. Particular attention will be paid to current issues and controversies where questions remain unanswered. Although focused on the experiences of women, this course is *not* for women only. By examining the psychological literature relevant to women both women and men can develop new insights, become aware of sexist biases, and begin to ask questions concerning gender in new ways. Prerequisites: PSYSC 100 and 241.

Required Text

Hyde, J.S. (1985). *Half the Human Experience: The Psychology of Women* (3rd ed.) Lexington, Massachusetts: D.C. Heath.

Requirements

1. Class attendance and participation. You are expected to attend class prepared for discussion of assigned materials. Persistent lack of preparation or participation constitutes unsatisfactory performance.

2. Gender Bias Analysis. You will be required to write two brief papers describing your analysis of gender bias in empirical research.

3. Position papers. You will be required to write 2 position papers. These are opinion papers, not research or term papers. My evaluation will be based on how well your position is presented.

4. Critical review and Evaluation. You will be required to submit a 7–10 page paper critically evaluating recent research relevant to a topic that concerns the psychology of women.

5. Exams. Exams may include multiple choice, short answer or essay items. Make-up exams will be given only for excused absences and must be completed within one week.

Date

Topic and Assignments

What is the psychology of women?

Psychological Research

Hyde, Chapter 1

McHugh, M.C., Koeske, R.D. and Frieze, I.H. (1986). Issues to consider in conducting nonsexist psychological research: A guide for researchers. *American Psychologist, 41*(8), 879–890.

Sexist bias in research

Designing nonsexist research

Historical Perspective

Hyde, Chapter 2

Furumoto, L. and Scarborough, E. (1986). "Placing women in the history of psychology: The first American women psychologists." *American Psychologist, 41*(1), 35–42.

Psychology and the woman question

Women in the history of psychology

Theoretical Perspectives

Hyde, Chapters 3 & 5

Freud, S. (1959). "Some psychological consequences of the anatomical distinction between the sexes." *Collected Papers, 5,* 186.

Bem, S.L. (1983). "Gender Schema theory and its implications for child development: Raising gender-aschematic children in a gender-schematic society." *Signs: Journal of Women in Culture and Society. 8*(4), 598–616.

Freud on women

Neo-psychoanalytic revisions

Sociobiology

Social Learning Theory/Cognitive theory

(Contracts due)

MSRI paradigm

Exam I

Sex Roles

Hyde, Chapter 4

Deaux, K. (1984). "From individual differences to social categories: Analysis of a decade's research on gender." *American Psychologist, 39*(2), 105–116.

Masculinity, Femininity and Androgyny

Influence of Stereotypes

Gender Differences

Hyde, Chapters 6, 8, 9

Linn, M.C. (1986). "Meta-analysis of studies of gender differences: Implications and further directions. In J. S. Hyde and M. C. Linn" *The Psychology of Gender: Advances through meta-analyses.* pp. 210–231. Baltimore: Johns Hopkins University Press.

Gilligan, C. (1979). "Woman's place in man's life cycle."

Harvard Educational Review, 49(4), 431–446.

The meaning and measurement of gender difference

The abilities of women and men

The behavior of women and men

Fear of success

In a different voice

Women and language

Socialization

Hyde, Chapter 7

Baruch, G.K.; Brenner, L.; Barnett, R.C. (1987). "Women and gender in research on work and family stress." *American Psychologist, 42,* 130–136.

Nonmaternal care

Women & employment

Single mothers

Biological influence

Hyde, Chapter 10

Grief, E.S. and Ulman, K.J. (1982). "The psychological impact of menarche on early adolescent females: A review of the literature." *Child Development, 53,* 1413–1430.

Biology and gender differences

Menarche, Menstruation, and Menopause

Exam II

Health Issues

Hyde, Chapters 11 & 14

Walsh, M.R. (1987). "Does Abortion Cause Psychological Harm to Women?" *The Psychology of Women: Ongoing Debates.* pp. 3787–408. New Haven: Yale University Press.

Women and Health

Abortion

Learned helplessness

Eating Disorders

Victimization of women

Hyde, Chapters 15 & 16

Walsh, M.R. (1987). "Is Pornography Harmful to Women?" *The Psychology of Women: Ongoing Debates.* pp. 427–460. New Haven: Yale University Press.

Greene, B. (1986). Bar wars. *Esquire, Nov,* 61–62.

Walker, L.E. & Browne, A. (1985). Gender and victimization by intimates. *Journal of Personality, 53*(2), 179–195.

Discrimination and sexual harassment

Rape and sexual assault

Battered women

Pornography

Sexual Issues

Hyde, Chapters 12 & 13

"Being a Lesbian."

Female sexuality

Lesbianism

(Projects Due)

The importance of power

Relationships and Sexuality

Looking to the Future

Hyde, Chapter 17

Harrison, B.G. (1981). "What do women want? Feminism and its future." *Harper's, Oct,* 39–48, 53–58.

Betty Friedan: The second wave

What do women want?

Grading Guidelines

A. Demonstrates outstanding ability to critically evaluate and integrate course material. Masters assigned work, but shows independent initiative.

B. Mastery of assigned material. Ability and initiative to fulfill more than basic requirements.

C. Fulfills basic requirements of course. Meets deadlines, adequate exam performance.

D. Below basic requirements. Persistent lack of preparation.

F. Unsatisfactory in either quality or quantity.

Important note: Plagiarism and other forms of cheating will not be tolerated. Those who indulge in this behavior will received failing grade for that assignment and will be referred to the Dean of Students Office for further disciplinary action.

Guidelines for Gender Bias Analysis

1. Choose a topic of interest to you that concerns the psychology of women.

2. Locate a recent article that describes an empirical study concerning that topic.

3. Briefly summarize the study.

4. Do an analysis of gender bias in this research.

5. Revise the research to meet the standards of gender fair research

6. Attach the complete reference (in APA style) and a photocopy of this articles' abstract.

Guidelines for Project

1. Choose a topic of interest to you that concerns the psychology of women.

2. Locate a literature review from a reputable journal that was published between 1970 and 1985. (Consult psychological Abstracts and the heading Literature Review)

3. Complete the REVIEW CONTRACT. Submit 2 copies of the contract and 1 copy of the article to the instructor.

4. Upon approval of the instructor, summarize the author's major points. These should include:
   A. Justification for research in this area
   B. Problems in the literature
   C. Conclusion
   D. Predictions or suggestions for future research
   (Maximum of 2 pages)

5. Locate at least 3 more recent articles from reputable journals that address this area of research. These can include either descriptions of studies or articles concerning conceptual issues. (Obviously, these articles should not have been covered in the review.)

6. Integrate these findings with those of the review. Are the new findings consistent or inconsistent with earlier findings? Are the new findings conceptualized in a different way? Do the new findings point out problems in the review? Do the new findings show a bias in the review? Have there been methodological changes? etc. (A *brief* description of each study may be necessary here.)
   (Maximum of 3 pages)

7. Based on your new knowledge, critically evaluate this area of research. What problems do you see? What are the most important issues? Where does the field appear to be headed? Is it headed in the right direction? How accurate were the reviewers' predictions? etc. Do more than report what the author suggests. This is your chance to make a contribution!
   (Approximately 1 page)

8. Reference List—please use APA style.

Syllabus III: Ellen Kimmel

University of South Florida

Leadership development in Women

Purpose: The seminar will review the agencies of influence that historically have enhanced or inhibited women's achievement of leadership roles in American society. Both internal psychological barriers and external legal, social and cultural barriers will be treated and strategies for overcoming these examined. Emphasis will be on the psychological processes underlying women's success and failures in positions of formal authority and sex differences (alleged or real) in role performance.

Assignments & Evaluation

Class Activity: Each participant in the seminar will read independently and make regular contributions based on this reading on the current class topic. As much as possible, bring your contribution to the class (*i.e.*, a copy of the selection-article, book segment, etc.) so it will be available to other participants. For the group to coalesce, it is important that every effort be made to attend regularly and join in the experiential activities that will occur during some classtime. Suggestions for seminar activities are greatly welcomed, and you are urged to try out your skills as a session/activity leader.

Book Review: For each session, at least one person will report on a book relating to the topic. The report should be informal and may take 20–30 minutes to both report and lead discussion/answer questions. A short written review that briefly abstracts the main elements and then evaluates the book in light of current literature should be turned in at the time of reporting.

Major Project: DUE DECEMBER 1 (3pm). Should you anticipate a problem, please mail the paper to arrive by that date. I contract to return these by the last class session. Possible types of projects include:

- Library research paper/review of literature. A 15–20 page review based on books and articles on any related topic (whether specifically listed or not). I do request that you clear the topic with me as a protection for you.

- Research proposal. Here, you may do a narrower literature review as preparation for designing a study in this area. Such a project would look like a thesis proposal with the introduction and method section (including hypotheses).

- Case study. You might wish to select a local woman leader in some field, such as business, education, politics, etc. and use her career development as the basis for a case. I have materials on case writing from the business standpoint and clinical case studies (*e.g.*, Erikson's on Ghandi) could also serve as a model.

- Design of an intervention strategy. Here you might put yourself in the place of an Organizational Development person working with or for an organization whose responsibility is to increase the number of women leaders through training or policy or procedural changes.

- Conduct and write up a data collection activity on a relevant question. This project might be likened to a pilot study one would do prior to a dissertation.

- Your invention.

Please use me as a resource person if you are so inclined in the development and completion of your project. Needless to say, the goal is to make it as meaningful or even useful to you as possible, not simply an exercise. APA style is the one I'm most familiar with, but any format is acceptable so long as you are consistent. Please type them, but do not spend time and money in unnecessary "beautification".

The relative weights of the assignments are as follows:

25% Book review and oral report

75% Project and oral report

The course may be taken S/U if your program permits it. Just inform me at some point.

Schedule

TOPIC	*READING*
Introduction to Course/Topic Selection	
Leadership & Women Overview 3pm "Accomplished Women"	

Agents for Development:
    Family & School
  3pm "Is a Career in Management
for You?"
	Monteaguda:
	(Sex Equity in Education

Agents for Development: Law & Media	

Role of Professional/Trade/Union/
    Political Organization
  3pm "Women's Rights in the U.S."
  5pm "Productivity and the
Self-Fulfilling Prophecy"
	Schwarz: *Women and
	      Educational Leadership*
	Alder: *Women in Academe*

Psychology of Women:
    Achievement, Attribution and Power
  3pm Rose Hill: "The Story of 'O'"
	Krug: *Cinderella Complex*

Psychology continued: Imposter Phen./Sex Typing of Occupations/etc.	Belge: *The Competent Woman*

Managerial Women/Sex Differences in
    Leadership Style
  3pm "Leadership: Style or
Circumstance"
	Sutherland: *Games Mother Never
	        Taught You*
	Whitney: *The New Executive Woman*

Strategies for Developing Women
    Leaders
  3pm "Women in Management: Threat
or Opportunity"
	Harris: *Men & Women of the
	Corporations*

Strategies Cont: Networking and Mentoring	Hannas: *Networking*

Career Achievement & Women's Life
  Cycle
	Ellenburg: *The Second Stage*
	Godard: *Two Career Couple*,
	       (Hall & Hale)
	Bailey: *Working Couples*, Rapoport)

Language: A Powerful Barrier	Hatcher: *Words & Women*
Project Reports — PROJECTS DUE	
Project Reports & Wrap-up 5pm "You Pack Your Own Chute"	

Syllabus IV: Michele A. Paludi

Hunter College

Psychology of Women
Course Description I

In this course we will discuss issues in the psychology of women from a life-span developmental psychology perspective. We will highlight continuities and discontinuities in the socialization of achievement, work, friendships and romantic relationships. In addition, we will discuss physical changes accompanying puberty and menopause and the psychological impact these changes have for women. Special topics include employed mothers and day care, eating disorders, and gender role transcendence. We will discuss the ways socioeconomic class, race, and ethnicity impact on issues in the psychology of women. And, we will become familiar with several psychological tests used to measure femininity and masculinity in girls and women.

A series of presentations and discussions will be the vehicle for sharing information in the course. I will distribute outlines of discussion topics, a bibliography for each topic, and lists of organizations dealing with girls' and women's mental health, physical health, achievement, victimization, and relationships.

I look forward to discussing the psychology of women with you this semester!

Readings
Text

Lott, B. (1987). *Women's lives: Themes and variations in gender learning.* Monterey, CA Brooks/Cole.

Articles (To be distributed in class

Witt: The two worlds of Native women

Fujitomi & Wong: The new Asian-American woman

Garcia-Bahne: La Chicana and the Chicano family

Malveaux: You have struck a rock: A note on the status of Black women in South Africa

Anderson-Kulman & Paludi: Working mothers and the family context: Predicting positive coping

Bem: Gender schema theory

Polivy & Herman: Dieting and binging

60

Evaluation

I will distribute three take-home essays tests throughout the semester. One will deal with the childhood unit, one for adolescence and young adulthood, and one for the unit on middle and older adulthood. There will be no cumulative final. You will have a choice of answering 2 out of 5 essays in each exam. Please limit your responses to 3 pages per essay. This requirement is for graduating seniors as well as students not graduating this semester.

I will assign points for each of the essay tests and assign final grades according to the following table:

Requirement	Points Each	Number	Total
Exams	100	3	300

270–300 : A
240–269 : B
210–239 : C
180–209 : D
Below 180 : F

Schedule of Discussion Topics

Topic	Readings
Orientation	Lott:3–12

Which woman do you admire the most? Why?

Topic	Readings
Sexist and Nonsexist language	
How girls learn about gender	Lott: 50–67
Continued	
Female infant and childhood development	Lott 28–49
Measuring girls' femininity and masculinity	
Discussion: Infancy and childhood	
Special Topic: Employed mothers and day care	Anderson-Kulman & Paludi
Female adolescent development: Physical changes	Lott: 85–100
Cognitive development in adolescence and young adulthood	Lott: 68–84

Achievement in adolescence and young adulthood for women	Lott: 213–239 Witt Malveaux
Adolescent and young adulthood: Relationships	Lott: 120–146 Fujitomi & Wong
Violence against adolescent and young adult women	Lott: 147–170
Measurement of femininity and masculinity in adolescence and young adulthood	

Special topic: Eating disorders

Middle and older adulthood Physical changes	Lott: 282–288
Issues in adjustment	Lott: 261–280
Relationships for women in middle and older adulthood	Lott: 288–190 Garcia-Bahne
Androgyny in middle and older adulthood?	Lott: 240–260

Special topic: Gender role transcendence

Discussion: Middle and older adulthood

Which woman do you admire the most? Why?

Open discussion

Valuing what is female and feminine	Lott: 294–312

Course (W)rap-up

Anderson-Kulman, R., & Paludi, M.A. (1986). Working mothers and the family context: Predicting positive coping. *Journal of Vocational Behavior, 28,* 241–253.

Fujitomi, I., & Wong, D. (1986). The new Asian-American woman. In S. Gonsalves (Ed.), *Readings on minority women: Interdisciplinary perspectives.* Action, MA: Copley.

Garcia-Bahne, B. (1986). LaChicana and the Chicano family. In S. Gonsalves (Ed.), *Readings on minority women: Interdisciplinary perspectives.* Action, MA: Copley.

Malveaux, J. (1986). You have struck a rock: A note on the status of black women in South Africa: In S. Gonsalves (Ed.), *Readings on minority women: Interdisciplinary perspectives.* Action, MA: Copley.

Polivy, J., & Herman, C.P. (1985). Dieting and binging: A causal analysis. *American Psychologist, 40,* 193–201.

Witt, S. (1986). The two worlds of women. In S. Gonsalves (Ed.), *Readings on minority women: Interdisciplinary perspectives.* Action, MA: Copley.

Bem, S.L. (1983). Gender schema theory and its implications for child development: Raising gender-aschematic children in a gender-schematic society. *Signs, 8,* 598–616.

Psychology of Women
Course Description II

Text:

Scarborough, E., & Furumoto, L. (1987). Untold lives: The first generation of American women psychologists. New York: Columbia University Press.

Articles (to be distributed in class)

Russo, N.F., & Denmark, F.L. (1987). Contributions of women to psychology. *Annual Review of Psychology, 39,* 279–298.

Doyle, J., & Paludi, M.A. (in press). *Sex and Gender.* Dubuque: William C. Brown Publishers.

Chapter 1: Overview

Chapter 9: Education and work

Jacklin, C.N. (1989). Female and male: Issues of gender. *American Psychologist, 44,* 127–133.

Hoffman, L. W. (1989). Effects of maternal employment in the two-parent family. *American Psychologist, 44,* 283–292.

Paludi, M.A., & Barickman, R. (in press). Sexual harassment of students: Victims of the college experience. In E. Viano (Ed.), *Victimology: An international perspective.* New York: Springer.

Course Description:

This semester we will discuss issues in the psychology of women from a biographical perspective of the first women psychologists, namely: Mary Calkins, Millicent Shinn, Ethel Puffer, Margaret Washburn, and Christine Ladd-Franklin. As we discuss the biographies of these women we will have an opportunity to examine our own lives and realities as well. Specifically, we will focus on the following issues in women's lives: integrating a career and family life, responsibilities for the care of children and aging parents, and discrimination in education and work. We will supplement the biographical material with research reports related to the topics under discussion.

Evaluation

There will be two requirements for this course: (1) a biographical sketch of a woman psychologist and (2) take-home essay tests.

Biographical Sketch. I am inviting you to do some biographical detective work on a woman psychologist. I would like you to provide the following information:

Date of Birth
Birth Name
Siblings
Education Experience
Barriers to Meeting Career Goals
Lifestyle Choice
Mentors in Graduate School
Topic(s) of Research

I have put together a list of women psychologists. You may select a woman from this list or choose another one you have read about. This list is attached to the syllabus. I encourage you to collaborate with another person in class on your biographical sketch.

We will display the information we collect about women psychologists in the psychology department!

Take-Home Essays. There will be two take-home essay tests that integrate the material from the reading, our discussions, presentations, and your personal experience. You will have a choice of responding to 2 out of 5 essays in each exam.

I will assign grades according to the following table:

Requirement	Number	Points Each	Total
Biographical Sketch	1	100	100
Exams	2	100	200

270–300 : A
240–269 : B
210–239 : C
180–209 : D
Below 180 : F

I look forward to discussing the psychology of women with you this semester. If I may be of assistance to you, please call and/or visit me in my office hours or at class time.

Schedule of Discussions

Topic	Readings
Orientation to Class	S&F: 1–13; 153–173
Sex and gender similarities and differences: Infancy and childhood	Jacklin
Adolescence and young adulthood	
Middle and older adulthood	
Psychology constructs the female: Research methodology	D&P: chpt. 1
Women psychologists: Hidden from view	Russo & Denmark S&F: 133–152
Exam 1	
Education of Women	D&P: chpt. 9
Mary Calkins	S&F: 17–51
Family Responsibilities Millicent Shinn	S&F: 53–69
Integrating Career and Lifestyle	Hoffman
Ethel Puffer	S&F: 72–90
Gatekeepers	Paludi & Barickman
Margaret Washburn	S&F: 91–107
Christine Ladd-Franklin	S&F: 109–129
Exam 2 To the present	S&F: 175–186; 187–201
Biographical Sketches	
Biographical sketches Course (W)rap-up	

Women Psychologists:

I have listed a few psychologists here. You may select one from this list or another one you have read about.

Mamie Phipps Clark
Eleanor Maccoby
Janet Taylor Spence
Maria Montessori
Anna Freud
Mary Cover Jones
Nancy Bayley
Leta Hollingworth
Carolyn Sherif
Inez Prosser
Helen Thompson Wooley
Florence Goodenough
June Etta Downey
Brenda Milner
Beatrice Lacey
Eleanor Gibson
Anne Anastasi
Dorthea Jameson
Leona Tyler
Karen Horney
Melanie Klein
Helene Deutsch
Martha Bernal
Ruth Howard
Sandra Bem
Christiana Morgan
Margaret Harlow
Tracy Kendler
Matina Horner
Barbara Strudler Wallston
Nancy Datan
Inge Broverman

Psychology of Women:
Course Description III

Texts

Walsh, M.R. (Ed.) (1987). *The psychology of women: Ongoing debates.* New Haven: Yale University Press.

Rothenberg, P.S. (Ed.) (1988). *Racism and Sexism: An integrated study.* New York: St. Martin's Press.

Special Issue of *Psychology of Women Quarterly: Hispanic Women and Mental Health.*

Course Description:

Psychology has nothing to say about what women are really like, what they need and what they want, essentially, because psychology does not know.

It has been 20 years since Naomi Weisstein wrote these words. In that time the field of the psychology of women has corrected the androcentric bias in psychology noted by Weisstein. The field has grown to the extent that several major textbooks have been written, most recently by Margaret Matlin, Bernice Lott, Mary Roth Walsh, Janet Hyde, and Susan Basow. And, currently Florence Denmark and Michele Paludi are preparing the handbook on the psychology of women.

In this course we will discuss issues related to the psychology of women, for example, achievement, interpersonal relationships, victimization, day care, health, and adjustment. We will integrate the scholarship on women of color and white women in our discussions of these topics within the context of socioeconomic class. The readings and discussions will focus on similarities and distinctiveness among Native American women, Asian women, Black women, Hispanic women, White women, and women in Third World countries.

A series of presentations and discussions will be the major vehicle for sharing information in this course. We will also have the opportunity to view some major films and videos on the topics under discussion.

Evaluation

Your grade will be based on the completion of two requirements: (1) take-home essay questions and (2) a character analysis.

The essay questions will be based on the readings assigned for the course in addition to discussions we will have in class. The questions will ask you to integrate the material from the readings, presentations, and personal experiences.

The character analysis will consist of a 5–10 page paper outlining two–three major issues in the psychology of women a fictional or real woman has experienced. Some possible women to select for this character analysis include:

woman friend, family member, self (if you are a woman)

woman characters from:
> Desert Hearts
> Cosby Show
> The Color Purple
> Madame Butterfly
> Growing Pains
> Three's Company
> Moonlighting
> Nuts
> Chorus Line
> any Soap Opera, e.g., All My Children
> Hannah and her Sisters
> Bull Durham
> Fatal Attraction
> She's Gotta Have it

Some issues to consider writing about in your character analysis: relationships among women; sexuality; mother-daughter relationship; career vs. home issues; victimization experiences; eating disorders.

Grading

I will assign points for each of the requirements. These points will be converted to a grade as illustrated below.

Requirement	Number	Points Each	Total
Essays	10	10	100
Character Analysis	1	100	100

> 180–200 = A
> 160–179 = B
> 140–159 = C
> 120–139 = D
> Below 120 = F

Other Considerations

I am looking forward to discussing the psychology of women with you this semester. Please call and/or visit me in my office if I may be of assistance to you.

Topics	*Corresponding Readings*
An Invitation to Study the Psychology of Women: Orientation to Course	Rothenberg: pp. 1–8
History of the Field of the Psychology of Women	Chehrazi; Lerman (in Walsh) Vazquez-Nuttall, Romero-Garcia, DeLeon (in PWQ) Rothenberg: pp. 20–21 Hess, Markson, & Stein (in Rothenberg)
Women in the History of Psychology	
Teaching the Psychology of Women	Moore (in Rothenberg)
In a Different Moral Voice? Toward an Ethic of Care	Gilligan; Colby & Damon (in Walsh)
Is Androgyny the Solution?	Bem; Bem (in Walsh) Ferguson (in Rothenberg)
Should Mothers Work Outside Home?	White; O'Connell, Chodorow, Rossi (in Walsh) Amaro, Russo, Johnson (in PWQ)
Women and Achievement: Challenging the Assumptions	Horner; Paludi; Benbow & Stanley; Eccles & Jacobs (in Walsh) Safran (in Rothenberg) Rothenberg: pp. 69–75 Malveaux (in Rothenberg) Kelly (in Rothenberg)
Personal Choices and Social Scripts	Gartress; Socarides; Osofsky & Osofsky; Loal, McGettigan, & Bucy (in Walsh) deSnyder (in PWQ)
Women's Health Issues	Dalton; Koeske; Budoff, McKinlay & McKinlay (in Walsh) Foley (in Rothenberg) Squire (in Rothenberg)
Psychological Adjustment	Gore; Johnson; Shainess; Caplan (in Walsh) Canino, et al (in PWQ) Russo, Amaro, Winter (in PWQ) Espin (PWQ)
Victimization of Women	Green; Malamuth (in Walsh) Eason (in Rothenberg)

The Future of the Psychology of Women   Rothenberg: pp. 376–390

Balancing the Psychology Curriculum for   Lorde (in Rothenberg)
Sex, Race, Ethnicity, and Class

Course (W)rap-up

Part 2
Foundations

2

Feminist and Sex-Fair Methodologies

Sample outline

Science: an androcentric and antifemale institution
Value-free *vs* value-laden research

Sources of bias in research

    Conceptual biases

    Models of reality

    Selection of research participants

    Experimenter effects

    Observer effects

    Statistical analyses

    Magnitude of differences

    Reporting of results

    Bias through linguistic patterns used in interpreting gender differences

    Biases of journals

    Bias in interpretations

Methodological/statistical considerations

    Demand characteristics

    Participants' awareness of study

    Control group

    Field *vs.* laboratory research

    Meta-analyses

    Sex-fair *vs.* feminist methodology

Projective hypothesis *vs.* perceptual hypothesis

Masculine bias of stimulus figure (*e.g.,* "IT" figure in IT Scale for Children)

Defining concepts of masculinity and femininity in terms of preconceived cultural standards

Cultural lag (*e.g.,* in item selection and classification as masculine or feminine)

Variation in scoring systems (*e.g.,* median split *vs.* *t*-score scoring of Bem Sex Role Inventory)

Male norming in test construction

Single-sex samples

Fidelity *vs.* bandwith

Social consequences of making Type I and Type II errors

Heterogeneous item contents

Validity issues

Theoretical *vs.* empirical typologies

Nomothetic *vs.* idiographic approaches

Aspects of gender-role identity

Gender-role preference

Gender-role adoption

Gender-role orientation

Gender-role identification

Attitudes toward gender roles

Knowledge of sex-determined role standards

Measurement of Gender-Role Identity

Additional tests may be found in Beere, C.A. (1979). *Women and Women's Issues: A Handbook of Tests and Measures.* San Francisco: Jossey-Bass. Tests cover the following topics: gender roles, gender stereotypes, somatic and sexual issues, gender-role prescriptions, children's gender roles, gender knowledge, marital and parental roles, employee roles, multiple roles, attitudes toward women's issues.

Gender-role preference

   IT Scale for Children (Brown, 1956)

   Toy Preference Test (DeLucia, 1963)

   Play Test (Rosenberg & Sutton-Smith, 1964)

   Children's Gender-Role Preference Scale (Paludi, 1980)

Gender-role adoption

   Activity Preference Scale (Connor & Serbin, 1977)

Gender-role orientation

   Bem Sex Role Inventory (Bem, 1974)

Gender-role identification

   Draw-A-Person Test (Machover, 1949)

Attitudes toward gender roles

   Attitudes Toward Women Scale (Spence and Helmreich, 1972)

Knowledge of sex-determined role standards

   A Day with Anne and Peter (Paludi, *et al.*, 1984)

Sample references

Value-free versus value-laden research

Bart, P.B. (1970). "Sexism and social science: From the gilded cage to the iron case or the perils of Pauline." *Journal of Marriage and the Family, 48,* 435–446.

Burt, M. (1982, August). "Guidelines for nonsexist research: Implications for policy and policy research." Paper presented at the Annual Meeting of the American Psychological Association, New York, NY.

Fine, M. (1985). "Reflections on a feminist psychology of women: Paradoxes and prospects." *Psychology of Women Quarterly, 9,* 167–183.

Henley, N. (1986, August). "Feminist psychology and feminist theory." Paper presented at the American Psychological Association, Washington, DC.

Holmes, D.S., and Jorgenson, B.W. (1971). "Do personality and social psychologists study men more than women?" *Representative Research in Social Psychology, 2,* 71–76.

Lott, B. (1985). "The potential enrichment of social/personality research through feminist research and vice versa." *American Psychologist, 40,* 155–164.

McKenna, W., and Kessler, S.J. (1977). "Experimental design as a source of sex bias in social psychology." *Sex Roles, 3,* 117–128.

Quina, K. (1986). "Teaching research methods: A multidimensional feminist curricular transformation plan." Wellesley College Center for Research on Women. Working Paper No. 164.

Roberts, H. (Ed.) (1981). *Doing Feminist Research.* Boston: Routeldge & Kegan Paul.

Schwabacker, S. (1972). "Male *vs.* female representation in psychological research: An examination of the Journal of Personality and Social Psychology, 1970, 1971." *JSAS Catalog of Selected Documents in Psychology, 2,* 20–21.

Shields, S.A. (1975). "Functionalism, Darwinism, and the psychology of women: A study in social myth." *American Psychologist, 30,* 739–754.

Tangri, S.S., and Strasburg, G.L. (1979). "Can research on women be more effective in shaping policy?" *Psychology of Women Quarterly, 3,* 321–343.

Unger, R.K. (1979). "Toward a redefinition of sex and gender," *American Psychologist, 34,* 1085–1094.

Unger, R.K. (1981). "Sex as a social reality: Field and laboratory research." *Psychology of Women Quarterly, 5,* 645–653.

Unger, R.K. (1983). "Through the looking glass: No wonderland yet!" *Psychology of Women Quarterly, 8,* 9–32.

Wittig, M.A. (1985). "Metatheoretical dilemmas in the psychology of gender." *American Psychologist, 40,* 800–811.

Methodological/statistical considerations

Brannon, R. (1974, August). "Feminist ideology and hard nosed methodology." Paper presented at the Meeting of the American Psychological Association, New Orleans.

Brannon, R. (1978). "Measuring attitudes (toward women and otherwise): A methodological critique." In J. Sherman and F. Denmark (Eds.), *The Psychology of Women: Future Directions in Research.* New York: Psychological Dimensions.

Brannon, R. (1981). "Current methodological issues in paper-and-pencil measuring instruments." *Psychology of Women Quarterly, 5,* 618–627.

Constantinople, A. (1973). "Masculinity-femininity: An exception to a famous dictum." *Psychological Bulletin, 80,* 389–407.

Denmark, F.L. Russo, N.F., Frieze, I.H. and Sechzer, J. (1988). "Guidelines for avoiding sexism in psychological research." *American Psychologist, 43,* 582–585.

Eagly, A. (1978). "Sex differences in influenceability." *Psychological Bulletin, 85,* 86–116.

Eagly, A., and Carli, L.L. (1981). "Sex of researchers and sex-typed communications as determinants of sex differences in influenceability: A meta-analysis of social influence studies." *Psychological Bulletin, 90,* 1–20.

Golub, S. (1986, August). "Women's research—women's lives." Paper presented at the American Psychological Association, Washington, DC.

Grady, K.E. (1981). "Sex bias in research design." *Psychology of Women Quarterly, 5,* 628–636.

Graham, D.L., and Rawlings, E.I. (1980, June). "Teaching an emerging feminist research methodology." Paper presented at the annual meeting of the National Women's Studies Association, Bloomington, IN.

Hyde, J.S. (1981). "How large are cognitive gender differences? A meta-analysis using r^2 and d." *American Psychologist, 36,* 892–901.

Hyde, J.S. (1984). "How large are gender differences in aggression? A developmental meta-analysis." *Developmental Psychology, 20,* 722–736.

Hyde, J.S. (1986, August). "Meta-analysis: What has it done for feminist psychology?" Paper presented at the American Psychological Association, Washington, DC.

Longino, H.E. (1986). *Can There be a Feminist Science?* Wellesley College Center for Research on Women. Working Paper No. 163.

Parlee, M.B. (1981). "Appropriate control groups in feminist research." *Psychology of women Quarterly, 5,* 637–644.

Sherif, C.W. (1979). "Bias in psychology." In J.A. Sherman and E.T. Beck (Eds.), *The Prism of Sex: Essay in the Sociology of Knowledge.* Madison: University of Wisconsin Press.

Unger, R.K. (1983). "Through the looking glass: No wonderland yet!" *Psychology of Women Quarterly, 8,* 9–32.

Wallston, B.S. (1981). "What are the questions in psychology of women: A feminist approach to research." *Psychology of Women Quarterly, 5,* 597–617.

Wallston, B.S. (1983). "Overview of research methods." In J. Writenberg and B.L. Richardson (Eds.), *Sex Role Research: Measuring Social Change.* New York: Praeger.

Wallston, B.S., and Grady, K.E. (1985). "Integrating the feminist critique and the crisis in social psychology: Another look at research methods." In V.E. O'Leary, R.K. Unger, and B.S. Wallston (Eds.), *Women, Gender, and Social Psychology.* Hillsdale, J.J.: Erlbaum.

Worell, J. (1978). "Sex roles and psychological well-being: Perspectives on methodology." *Journal of Consulting and Clinical Psychology, 46,* 777–791.

Sources of bias in research

Carlson, E.R., and Carlson, R. (1960). "Male and female subjects in personality research." *Journal of Abnormal and Social Psychology, 61,* 482–483.

Constantinople, A. (1973). "Masculinity/femininity: An exception to a famous dictum?" *Psychological Bulletin, 80,* 389–407.

Carai, J.E., & Scheinfeld, A. (1968). "Sex differences in mental and behavioral traits." *Genetic Psychology Monographs, 17,* 169–299.

Gelles, R., and Pedrick-Cornell, C. (1981). "Watch on the right: Beware the "research shows" ploy." *Ms.,* June, 100.

Greenwald, A.G. (1975). "Consequences of prejudice against the null hypothesis." *Psychological Bulletin, 82,* 1–20.

Harmon, L. (1973). "Sex bias in interest measurement." *Measurement and Evaluation in Guidance, 5,* 496–501.

Holmes, D.S., and Jorgensen, B.W. (1971). "Do personality and social psychologists study men more than women?" *Representative Research in Social Psychology, 2,* 71–76.

Keller, E.F. (1985). *Reflections on Gender and Science.* New Haven, Conn.: Yale University Press.

Koch, S. (1981). "The nature and limits of psychological knowledge: Lessons of a century qua 'science.'" *American Psychologist, 36,* 257–269.

McHugh, M.C., Koeske, R.D., and Frieze, I.H. (1986). "Issues to consider in conducting nonsexist psychological research." *American Psychologist, 41,* 879–890.

McKenna, W., and Kessler, S.J. (1977). "Experimental design as a source of sex bias in social psychology." *Sex Roles, 3,* 117–128.

Reardon, P., and Prescott, S. (1976). "Reexamination of male versus female representation in psychological research." *Catalog of Selected Documents in Psychology, 6*, 38.

Schwabcher, S. (1972). "Male *vs.* female representation in psychological research. *Journal Supplement Abstract Service, 2*, 20–21.

Signorella, M. (1981). "Subject selection and analyses for sex-related differences: 1968–1970 and 1975–1977." *American Psychologist, 36*, 988.

Unger, R.K. (1982). "Advocacy versus scholarship revisited: Issues in the psychology of women." *Psychology of Women quarterly, 7*, 5–17.

Weisstein, N. (1971). "Psychology constructs the female." In V. Gornick & B. Moran (Eds.), *Women in Sexist Society.* New York: Signet.

Measurement of gender-role identity

IT scale for children

Brinn, J., Kraemet, K., Warm, J.S., and Paludi, M.A. (1984). "Sex-role preferences in four age levels." *Sex Roles, 11*, 901–910.

Brown, D.G. (1956). "Sex-role preference in young children." *Psychological Monographs, 70*, No. 14 (Whole No. 421).

Brown, D.G. (1956). *The IT Scale for Children.* Missoula, MT: Psychological Test Specialists.

Brown, D.G. (1957). "Masculinity-femininity development in children." *Journal of Consulting and Clinical Psychology, 21*, 197–202.

Dickstein, E.B., and Seymour, M.W. (1977). "Effect of the addition of neutral items on IT scale scores." *Developmental Psychology, 13*, 79–80.

Lansky, L.M., and McKay, G. (1963). "Sex-role preferences of kindergarten boys and girls: Some contradictory results." *Psychological Reports, 13*, 415–421.

Paludi, M.A. (1981). "Sex-role discrimination among girls: Effect on IT Scale Scores." *Developmental Psychology, 17*, 851–852.

Paludi, M.A. (1982). "A comment on the misuse of the chi-square statistic in research using the IT scale for children." *Sex Roles: A Journal of Research, 8*, 791–793.

Reed, M.R., and Asbjornsen, W. (1968). "Experimental alteration of the IT scale in the study of sex-role preference." *Perceptual and Motor Skills, 26*, 15–24.

Sher, M.A., and Lansky, L.M. (1968). "The IT scale for children: Effects of variations in the sex-specificity of the IT figure." *Merrill-Palmer Quarterly, 14,* 323–330.

Thompson, N.L., & McCandless, B.R. (1970). "IT score variations by instructional style." *Child Development, 41,* 425–436.

Toy preference test

DeLucia, L. (1963). "The toy preferences test: A measure of sex-role identification." *Child Development, 34,* 107–117.

Play test

Rosenberg, B.G., and Sutton-Smith, B. (1964). "The measurement of masculinity and femininity in children: An extension and revalidation." *Journal of Genetic Psychology, 104,* 259–264.

Children's gender-role preference scale

Paludi, M.A. (1982, April). "The children's sex-role preference scale: Construction of a measuring instrument." Paper presented at the Convention of the Southwestern Society for Research in Human Development, Galveston, TX.

Gender-role adoption

Connor, J.M., and Serbin, L.A. (1977). "Behaviorally based masculine and feminine activity preference scales for preschoolers: Correlates with other classroom behaviors and cognitive tests." *Child Development, 48,* 1411–1416.

Gender-role orientation

Bem, S.L. (1974). "The measurement of psychological androgyny." *Journal of Consulting and Clinical Psychology, 42,* 155–162.

Bem, S.L. (1977). "On the utility of alternative procedures for assessing psychological androgyny." *Journal of Consulting and Clinical Psychology, 45,* 196–205.

Spence, J.T., & Helmreich, R.L. (1979). "On assessing 'androgyny.'" *Sex Roles, 5,* 721–738.

Gender-role identification

Machover, K. (1949). Personality Projection in the Drawing of the Human Figure. Springfield, IL: Thomas.

Paludi, M.A. (1978). "Machover revisited: Impact of sex-role orientation on sex sequence on the Draw-A-Person test." *Perceptual and Motor Skills, 47,* 713–714.

Paludi, M.A., and Bauer, W.D. (1979). "Impact of sex of experimenter on the Draw-a-Person test." *Perceptual and Motor Skills, 49,* 456–458.

Farylo, B. and Paludi, M.A. (1985). "Research with the Draw-a-Person test: Conceptual and methodological issues." *Journal of Psychology, 119,* 575–580.

Attitudes toward gender roles

Spence, J.T., and Helmreich, R. (1972). "The attitudes toward women scale." *JSAS Catalog of Selected Documents in Psychology, 2,* 66.

Spence, J.T., and Helmreich, R. (1978). *Masculinity and Femininity.* Austin: University of Texas Press.

Spence, J.T., Helmreich, R., and Stapp, J. (1973). "A short version of the attitudes toward women scale (AWS)." *Bulletin of the Psychonomic Society, 2,* 219–220.

Knowledge of Sex-Determined Role Standards

Paludi, M.A., Geschke, D., Smith, M., and Strayer, L.A., (1984). "The development of a measure of preschoolers' knowledge of sex-determined role standards." *Child Study Journal, 14,* 171–183.

Sample discussion questions

- Discuss Mary Brown Parlee's (1979) claim that "one hallmark of feminist research in any field seems to be the investigator's continual testing of the plausibility of the work against her own experience."

- Discuss whether research that reports statistically significant gender differences have practical significance.

- Discuss how the concept of overlapping normal curves is important in understanding gender-role research considering the fact that it undermines the basis of discriminatory regulations and laws.

- Offer three examples of how traditionally empirically based science can be thought of as having an androcentric bias.

- Discuss the ways in which methodological biases in research can be traced to conceptual biases on the part of the author(s).

- Discuss how the following research designs used in studying gender differences have serious limitations: correlational studies, retrospective questionnaires, self-reports.

- Discuss Stephanie Shield's (1975) comment that interpretation of facts has sometimes determined the facts themselves.

- Describe the bias against non-White, non-middle class individuals that has existed in psychology.

- Discuss the "male as normative" in theory construction in psychology. Be sure to address the issue that theories based solely or primarily on boys and men have been generalized to "people in general."

- How may observer and experimenter biases be lessened?

- Describe the heterosexist bias that exists in research on romantic relationships and childrearing.

- What are some feminist correctives to the following research biases: conceptual bias, selection of research participants, reporting results, bias through linguistic patterns used in interpreting gender differences.

Suggestions for sex-fair research

By M.C. McHugh, R.D. Koeske, and I.H. Frieze, *American Psychologist*, 1986, 41. Reprinted here with permission by the American Psychological Association.

Avoiding excessive confidence in traditional methods

1. Carefully examine the underlying values and assumptions in all research and state them explicitly.

2. Encourage the use of alternative and nonexperimental research methodologies directed toward exploration, detailed description, and theory generation as well as experimental and quasi-experimental approaches designed for hypothesis testing.

3. Engage in ongoing debate about the strengths and weaknesses of all research techniques, focusing attention on the capacities and limitations of experimental research as procedures for studying processes and systems and for permitting generalizations to particular contexts.

4. When undertaking literature reviews, examine past research for both methodological rigor and unexamined sexism in procedure or interpretation.

   a. Be aware of factors other than methodological soundness that may

84

influence the publishability or distribution of results.

b. Remember that the convergence of established findings with experience and the convergence of results based on different methods adds to their credibility; divergence should prompt renewed study.

Examining Explanatory Models

1. Exercise care in the terminology employed to describe or explain results in order to avoid: (a) confusing sex with gender; (b) confusing description with explanation and; (c) reducing complex or interactionist explanations to overly simple ones.

2. Consider all possible explanations for sex-related phenomena including social-cultural, biological, and situational factors.
   a. Consider alternative explanations even if they have not been investigated.
   b. Recognize that many consistently demonstrated sex-related behaviors may result from either consistent and pervasive cultural factors or biological factors. Often empirical tests differentiating competing explanations are unavailable.

3. Become aware of, consider, and devise studies of alternative and more complex models of causation.
   a. More detailed models that incorporate and specify relationships involving both physiological and sociocultural variables are needed.
   b. Increased effort should be directed toward developing common terminologies and providing more elaborate tests of competing explanatory models.

4. Avoid concluding or implying that a covariation between biology and behavior constitutes evidence for physiological causation if information on alternative or methodological interpretations is unavailable.

5. Take care in distinguishing between a general construct and the specific measures meant to operationalize it.
   a. Be careful to appropriately delimit the meaning of a concept before operationalizing it.
   b. Avoid operationalizing or defining constructs in a manner that is circular or that does not allow specific tests of expected linkages to sex or gender.

6. Any discussion of sex-related differences should avoid language that (a) implies biological or social causation not demonstrated in the research, (b) implies that the characteristic under study is possessed exclusively by one sex, (c) implies dispositional differences when situational factors

may explain the result, or (d) inappropriately implies than men's and women's responses fall on opposite ends of a single continuum.

7. Avoid errors in interpretation of data such as inferring the presence of a significant sex-related difference without conducting direct statistical comparisons or considering results of tests for sex-related differences without consideration of the magnitude of the effect or the degree of overlap between distributions.

8. Perform analyses for sex-related differences whenever such analyses are justified by a theoretical or conceptual framework of the study.

9. Journal editors should discourage the publication of studies in which the only significant finding is an unexpected "sex difference" and should insist instead on the replication of such findings.

10. Equal emphasis in publication should be given to findings of "sex similarities," rather than biasing journal policy toward findings of "sex differences."

Interpreting Without Bias

1. Carefully consider both the basis and the implications of the labels applied to individual traits and behaviors.

2. Do not label behaviors or traits as dysfunctional without any empirical demonstration of their dysfunctionality.
   a. Devote some attention to examining the positive consequences of behaviors that deviate from the status quo or from traditional gender roles.
   b. Specify the context or subpopulation appropriate to the interpretation of normative labels or statements.

3. Psychological analyses require not only the measurement of some pattern of behavior and/or cognition, but also descriptions and analysis of the situational context and the environment.
   a. Complete an analysis of the social context of the study in order to determine if overt or subtle forms of sex bias are present.
   b. Carefully consider the possible differential salience, familiarity, relevance, and/or meaning of the research task, stimuli, and/or dependent measures to male and female participants.
   c. Once the research plan is completed, learn from the research participants how they evaluated and interpreted the research contexts, and how they felt as events transpired.

4. Base conclusions regarding the behaviors and responses of males and females on research in multiple contexts in an attempt to understand situational influences on behavior. Exercise care in drawing conclusions from research based on limited contexts.

5. Consider the role(s) of the experimenter, confederate, target, and others present, as they impact on the response, performance, or behavior of the participants.
   a. When appropriate, incorporate multiple experimenters (confederates and targets) to allow for analysis of experimenter effects and/or counterbalancing.
   b. Vary the sex composition of the group to allow for analysis or counterbalancing of possible effects.

6. Make sure that the theoretical framework that form the body of psychological research are relevant to members of both sexes.

8. Try to ensure that topics of interest to women are given the resources and status accorded to topics of interest to men.
   a. Do not limit the content areas of psychological research by the degree to which they can be studied under a single paradigm.
   b. Try to make sure that the extent to which particular research topics are judged as basic versus applied, or nonclinical versus clinical, does not depend on the sex of the respondent used or the judged gender relevance of the topic.

9. Carefully examine the normative assumptions implicit in the choice of typical and atypical samples of males and females and avoid: (a) inappropriately generalizing to all members of a sex; (b) unintentionally introducing uncontrolled variables into male-female comparisons, and; (c) unwittingly comparing typical samples of one sex with atypical samples of the other.

Sample Exercises

Exercise:

Becoming Acquainted with the Library Resources on Women's Issues

Steps for Completing the Exercise:

1. Ask students to browse through the latest issues of *Psychology of Women Quarterly* and *Sex Roles.*

2. Have them answer the following questions about each of the issues they read:
   a. Who is the general editor of the journal?
   b. Who publishes the journal?
   c. What type of articles do the journals publish (*e.g.*, review, reports of research, theoretical articles)?

3. Ask students to select one research article from each journal and answer the following questions:
   a. What volume of the journal did you select?
   b. What is the full citation (in APA style) of the article?
   c. What question, problem, or hypothesis did the author(s) investigate?
   d. Why do you believe this topic is important? How does the author(s) say the topic relates to what has been published previously?
   e. Where was the study conducted?
   f. What instruments and techniques were used?
   g. Who was studied? Why?
   h. How did the author(s) summarize the observations?
   i. Did the findings turn out as anticipated? Why or why not?
   j. Pretend you have been asked to do a follow-up study to the one you have read. What would you do? Why?

Exercises

Library Resources in Women's Studies

Steps for Completing the Exercise:

Invite a librarian at your university or college library to come to class to discuss how to use the card category and discuss bibliographies and guides as well as indexes and abstracts on women's studies.

Exercise

Influence of Values on Science
(This exercise has been adapted from Vivian P. Makosky and is used here with her permission.)

Steps for Completing Proposal

1. You will need a stop watch, a needle with a small eye, spool of thread, a pair of small scissors.

2. Ask for five women students to come to the front of the classroom and thread a needle. Each woman has one trial, during which they are to: (1) pick up the needle and thread; (2) thread the needle; (3) tie a knot in the end of the thread; (4) cut the knot off again; (5) take out the thread, and; (6) replace the needle and thread on the desk. Tell the women they're doing fine. Time each trial, obtain the average.

3. Now ask five men to do the same task. As they approach the front of the room, indicate to them they probably won't do well, but that you appreciate their cooperation. Proceed as in step 3, except make consoling statements after each trial.

4. Compare average times. The women will win. Announce that this was a test of fine motor aptitude, that women are clearly superior, and therefore only women should be allowed to be neurosurgeons.

5. Have the class voice their objections to the study and your conclusion. List these on the board.

6. Discuss sources of sex bias in research in relation to the class comments.

Exercise

Sex Bias in Psychological Research

Steps for Completing the Exercise:

1. Ask students to find an article reporting empirical research in any field of psychology.

2. Have the students critique the article for the types of sex bias described in the following texts listed below:

Frieze, I.H., Parsons, J.E., Johnson, P.B., Ruble, D.N., and Zellman, G.L. (1978). *Women and Sex Roles: A Social Psychological Perspective.* NY: Norton.

Hyde, J.S. (1985). *Half the Human Experience.* Lexington, MA: D.C. Heath.

Process of Psychological Research

Theoretical model
  Hypothesis generation
  Research design
  Collect the data
  Statistical analyses
  Interpretation of data
  Publication of research
  Incorporation of research into scientific knowledge

Sources of Sex Bias

Biased model
  Biased questions
  Experimenter effects
  Observer effects
  Magnitude of effect not tested
  Biased interpretation
  Publication of only significant statistics
  Women considered less authoritative
  Selective use of research to conform to scientists' bias

3. Ask students to bring their critique to class. ask several to share their critiques with their classmates.

4. Discuss the importance of becoming sensitive to biases that may or may not be present when conducting as well as when reading research. Bring up feminist alternatives to the bias in psychological research.

Exercise:

Women Psychologists: Hidden From View?

Steps for Completing the Exercise:

1. Ask students to look through their introductory psychology textbooks and list classic experiments that are described.

2. Post the experimenters' name generated by the students. You may want to list others, *e.g.,* Harlow's contact comfort studies, Sherif's Robber's Cave experiment, Taylor's Manifest Anxiety Scale, Morgan and Murray's Thematic Apperception Test.

3. Ask students whether the experimenter is male or female.

4. Discuss how the use of surnames of psychologists may lead people to view researchers as male, especially if the research is in an area considered "masculine."

5. You may want to have students read articles about the misrepresentation of women in the history of psychology. Sample references are provided in this chapter.

6. Invite female psychologists from your department and/or neighboring colleges and universities to your class to describe their research, clinical, and teaching interests.

7. If you are a woman, spend class time sharing your own research program with your students.

Exercise:

Research Proposal

Steps for Completing the Exercise:

1. Tell students to pretend that the Psychology of Women Foundation has just announced a program of research grants designed to foster our understanding of the psychology of women. These grants will be given on the basis of the proposals to be submitted.

2. Ask students to develop a research proposal for this program. Ask them to select an area in the psychology of women they wish to study.

3. Have students develop a list of at least 10 reports of original research in this area. Ask them to use *Psychological Abstracts* for this purpose.

4. Ask students to write a 15–20 page proposal including the following sections:
   a. Introduction: Why study is important, hypotheses to be developed
   b. Sample: Infants, children, adolescents, adults, ages, ethical concerns, permissions needed
   c. Procedures: Methods, time sampling involved, triangulation of methods, analyses
   d. Summary: Statement of how the project will benefit the psychology of women; interpretation of findings; proposal of subsequent studies
   e. Presentation: Oral presentation to colleagues in class

3

*Intracultural and Intercultural Similarities and Distinctiveness**

Sample Outline

Ethnocentrism and cultural relativism

Cultural universals and cultural variations in gender roles

Margaret Mead: *Sex and Temperament in Three Primitive Societies*
     Arapesh
     Mundugumor
     Tchambuli

American Indian Tribes
     Crow: Berdache
     Navajo and Mohave: Nadle
     Mohave: Alyha and Hwame

Changing gender roles
     Soviet Union
     Peoples Republic of China
     Scandinavian countries
     Israeli Kibbutz

Class distinctions: class *vs.* race explanations

Women of Color: Adaptation, achievement, health, and socialization of gender roles

Term "Third World Women" *vs.* "Women of Color" *vs.* Ethnic Minority Women

Dialectics of sex, gender-role, race, class, ethnicity

---

* Cultural Similarities and Distinctiveness Issues Are Presented Within All Chapters. A Separate Chapter is Devoted to these Concerns as Well.

  Additional information may be obtained from Michele Paludi and Darlene DeFour, Department of Psychology, Hunter College, 695 Park Avenue, New York, NY 10021.

93

Sample References

General

Almquist, E.M., and Wehrle-Einhorn, J.L. (1978). "The doubly disadvantaged: Minority women in the labor force." In A.H. Stromberg and S. Harkness (Eds.), *Women Working.* Palo Alto, Calif.: Mayfield.

Benedict, R. (1961). *Patterns of Culture.* Boston: Houghton Mifflin.

Blicksilver, E. (Ed.) (1978). *The Ethnic American Woman: Problems, Protests, Lifestyles.* Dubuque, IA: Kendall/Hunt.

Bronstein, P., and Quina, K. (Eds.). (1988). *Toward a Psychology of People: Resources for Gender and Sociocultural Awareness.* Washington, DC: American Psychological Association.

Cole, J. (Ed.) (1986). *All American Women: Lines that Divide, Ties that Bind.* New York: Free Press.

Duley, J.I., and Edwards, M.I. (1986). *The Cross-Cultural Study of Women.* New York: The Feminist Press.

Jacobs, S.E. (1974). *Women in Perspective: A Guide for Cross-Cultural Studies.* Urbana, IL: University of Illinois Press.

McNett, I., Taylor, L., and Scott, L. (1985). "Minority women: Doubly disadvantaged." In A.G. Sargent (Ed.), *Beyond Sex Roles.* St. Paul, Minn.: West.

Mead, M. (1935/1963). *Sex and Temperament in Three Primitive Societies.* New York: Norton.

Munroe, R.H., Shimmin, H.S., and Munroe, R.L. (1984). "Gender understanding and sex role preference in four cultures." *Developmental Psychology, 20,* 673–682.

Reid, P., and Puryear, G.R. (1981). *Minority Women: Social and Psychological Inquiries.* New York: Holt, Rinehart, & Winston.

Simons, M.A. (1979). "Racism and feminism: A schism in the sisterhood." *Feminist Studies, 5,* 384–401.

Asian Women

Andors, P. (1983). *The Unfinished Liberation of Chinese Women: 1949–1980.* Bloomington: Indiana University.

Curtin, K. (1975). *Women in China.* New York: Pathfinder.

Fan, K.S. (1982). *Women in Southeast Asia: A Bibliography.* Boston, Mass.: G.K. Hall.

Keyes, S. (1984). "Sex differences in cognitive abilities and sex-role stereotypes in Hong Kong Chinese adolescents." *Sex Roles, 9,* 853–870.

Kristera, J. "On the women of China." *Signs, 1,* 57–82.

Lott, L.T., and Pian, C. (1979). *Beyond Stereotypes and Statistics: Emergence of Asian and Pacific American Women.* Washington, DC: Organization of Pan-Asian American Women.

Hispanic Women

Bauman, R.P. (1984). "A study of Mexican women's perceptions of factors that influence academic and professional goal attainment." *Dissertation Abstracts International, 45* (5–A), 1248.

Cabello-Argandona, R. (1975). *The Chicano: A Comprehensive Bibliographic Study.* Los Angeles, Calif.: Chicano Studies Center, University of California.

DeMonteflores, C. (1981). "Conflicting alliances: Therapy issues in Hispanic lesbians." *Catalyst, 12,* 33–44.

Diaz-Guerrero, R. (1977). "Mexican psychology." *American Psychologist, 32,* 934–944.

Espin, O. (1987). "Issues of identity in the psychology of Latina lesbians." In Boston Lesbians Psychologies Collective (Eds.) *Lesbian Psychologies: Explorations and Challenges.* Champaign, IL: University of Illinois Press.

Gonzalez, M.L., and Nezu, A. (1986, August). "Stress and acculturation in Cuban women." Paper presented at the American Psychological Association, Washington, DC.

HAPI, Hispanic American Periodicals Index (1975–present). Los Angeles, Los Angeles Latin American Center Publications.

Martinez, J.L. (Ed.) (1978). *Chicana Psychology.* New York: Academic Press.

Melville, M.B. (1980). *Twice a Minority: Mexican American Women.* Chicago, IL: University of Chicago Press.

Towns-Miranda, L. (1986, August). "Acculturation, sex-role traditionalism, and symptomatology among Puerto-Rican women." Paper presented at the American Psychological Association, Washington, DC.

Velez de Urrutia, Z. (1986). "Rape and after rape experience: An analysis of the role of social support system upon the recovery process of Puerto Rican women: 1983–1984." *Dissertation Abstracts International, 46* (9–A), 2813.

Zamudio, B. (198, August). "Factors which influence educational attainment among Mexican-American women." Paper presented at the American Psychological Association, Washington, DC.

Native American Women

Blackwood, E. (1984). "Sexuality and gender in certain native American tribes: The case of cross-gender." *Signs, 10,* 27–42.

Callender, C., and Kochems, L. (1983). "The north American berdache." *Current Anthropology, 24,* 443–470.

Forgey, D. (1974). "The institution of berdache among the North American Plains Indians." *Journal of Sex Research, 11,* 1–15.

Green, R. (1983). *Native American Women: A Contextual Bibliography.* Bloomington, IN: Indiana University Press.

Gridley, M.E. (1974). *American Indian Women.* New York: Hawthorn.

Witt, S.H. (1974). "Native American women today: Sexism and the Indian woman." *Civil Rights Digest,* 29–35.

Black Women

Beale, F. (1970). "Double jeopardy: To be Black and female." In T. Cade (Ed.) *The Black Woman: An Anthology.* New York: New American Library.

Brown, A., Goodwin, B.J., Hall, B.A., and Jackson-Lowman, H. (1985). "A review of psychology of women textbooks: Focus on the Afro-American woman." *Psychology of Women Quarterly, 9,* 29–38.

Dill, B.T. (1979). "The dialectics of Black womanhood." *Signs, 4,* 543–555.

Epstein, C.F. (1973, August). "Black and female: The double whammy." *Psychology Today,* 57.

Fleming, J. (1982). "Fear of success in Black male and female graduate students: A pilot study." *Psychology of Women Quarterly, 6,* 327–341.

Gump, J.P. (1978). "Reality and myth: Employment and sex role ideology in Black women." In J.A. Sherman and F. L. Denmark (Eds.) *The Psychology of Women: Future Directions of Research.* New York: Psychological Dimensions.

Hill, M. (1987). "Child rearing attitudes of Black lesbian mothers." In Boston Lesbian Psychologies Collective (Eds.) *Lesbian Psychologies: Explorations and Challenges.* Champaign, IL: University of Illinois Press.

Powell, L. (1986, August). "Mental status of Black women: A ten year study." Paper presented at the American Psychological Association, Washington, DC.

Richardson, M. (1980). *Black Women and Religion: A Bibliography.* Boston, Mass.: G.K. Hall.

Roberts, J.R. (1981). *Black Lesbians: An Annotated Bibliography.* Tallahassee, FL: Naiad Press.

Stovall-Hurdle, L. (1986, August). "Black women: Racism and psychotherapy." Paper presented at the American Psychological Association, Washington, DC.

Pamphlets, Special Issues, Bibliographies, Newsletters, Symposia

Pamphlets

> Africana Women's Studies
> 223 James P. Brawley Drive
> Atlanta University
> Atlanta, GA 30314

> National Network of Hispanic Women
> Center for Research on Women
> Stanford University
> P.O. Box 4223
> Stanford, CA 94305

> Cross-cultural Perspective and Women's Experiences
> Wheaton College
> Norton, MA 02766

> Black Re-Entry Females: Their Concerns and Needs
> Mildren Dalton Henry
> National Association for Women Deans, Administrators,
>   and Counselors
> 1325 18 Street, NW
> Suite 210
> Washington, DC 20036

Special Issues

Allen, R.L. (Ed.). (1981). "The best of the Black Scholar: The Black Woman." *The Black Scholar, 12* (6).

Allen, R.L. (Ed.). (1982). "The Black Woman II." Special Issue: *The Black Scholar, 13*(4–5).

Amaro, H., and Russo, N.F. (Eds.). (1987). "Hispanic women and mental health: Contemporary issues in research and practice." *Psychology of Women Quarterly, 11* (4).

Dudley, G.R., and Rawlins, M.R. (Eds.). (1985). "Psychotherapy with ethnic minorities." *Psychotherapy, 22* (2, Supplement).

Levinger, G. (Ed.) (1987). "Black employment opportunities: Macro and micro perspectives." *Journal of Social Issues.*

Murray, S.R., and Scott, P.B. (Eds.) (1981). "Special issue on Black women." *Psychology of Women Quarterly.*

Bibliographies

Fan, K.S. (1982). *Women in Southeast Asia: A Bibliography.* Boston: G.K. Hall.

Kessler, S. "Third world women in agriculture: Annotated bibliography." National Council for Research on Women, Sara Delano Roosevelt House, 47–49 East 65 Street, New York, NY 10021

Richardson, M. (1980). *Black Women and Religion: A Bibliography.* Boston, Mass.: G.K. Hall.

Symposium

American Psychological Association, 1986

Title: Toward an egalitarian psychology: Perspectives from five minorities

Chairperson: Arnold Kahn (James Madison University)

Panel: Adrienne Asch, Martha Bernal, Halford Fairchild, Harold Kooden, Martha Mednick

Organizations Serving Ethnic Minority Women

Organization	Address
Multicultural Women's Resource Center	Information Systems Development 1100 East 8 Street Austin, TX 78702
Mid-Atlantic Center for Race Equity	The American University 4900 Massachusetts Avenue, N.W. Washington, DC 20036
National Institute for Women of Color	1712 N Street, N.W. Washington, DC 20036
National Network of Minority Women in Science	Association for the Advancement of Science Office of Opportunities in Science 1776 Massachusetts Avenue, N.W. Washington, DC 20036
Asian Women United	170 Park Row #5A New York, NY 10038

Association of Black Women in Higher Education	30 Limerick Drive Albany, NY 12204
Black Career Women, Inc.	706 Walnut Street Suite 804 Cincinnati, OH 45202
American Council on Education	Office of Women in Higher Education 1 Dupont Circle, N.W. Suite 829 Washington, DC 20036
Liaison for Minorities and Women in Higher Education	U.S. Department of Education Office of Post Secondary Education 400 Maryland Avenue, S.W. Room 3022 Washington, DC 20202
National Chicano Council on Higher Education	600 West 28 Street Austin, TX 78705
Hispanic American Career Educational Resources, Inc.	115 West 30 Street Room 900 New York, NY 10001
Chicana Re-Entry Program	University of California Santa Barbara Educational Opportunities Program Chicanos and Others Building 406 Santa Barbara, CA 92106
Association for Cross-Cultural Education and Social Studies, Inc.	4340 East West Highway Suite 906 Bethesda, MD 20814
American Indian Women's Service League	617 Second Avenue Seattle, WA 98104
National Network of Hispanic Women	P.O. Box 4223 Stanford University Stanford, CA 94305
Indian Women United for Social Justice	P.O. Box 38743 Los Angeles, CA 90038
Asian Women's Health Project	Asian American Studies Center University of California Los Angeles, CA 90024
Center for Mexican Studies	University of Texas Austin, TX 78712

Additional information may be obtained from the Project on the Status and Education of Women, 1818 R Street, NW, Washington, DC 20009.

Audio-Visual Material

Title	Distributor	Description
La Opercion (Film)	The Cinema Guild	Describes female sterilization.
The Double Day (Film)	Tricontinental Films 333 Avenue of the Americas New York, NY 10014	Discusses role strain among employed mothers.
Suzanne, Suzanne (Film)	Third World Newsreel 335 W. 38th St. New York, NY 10018	Discusses drug abuse, alcoholism, and domestic violence in Black families.
The Confrontation: Latinas Fight Back Against Rape (Film)	Women Make Movies 225 Lafayette New York, NY 10012	Describes date rape.
Bottle Babies (Film)	NCC Audio-Visual-Room 860 475 Riverside Drive New York, NY 10115	Describes the impact of infant formula on women and children in Third World countries.
Naked Spaces: Living is Round (Film)	Women Makes Movies 225 Lafayette New York, NY 10012	Discusses ritual life in the rural environment of six West African countries.
Selbe: One Among Many (Film)	Women Makes Movies 225 Lafayette New York, NY 10012	Describes the social role and economic responsibility of women in African society
On Becoming a Woman: Mothers and Daughters Talking Together (Film)	Women Makes Movies 225 Lafayette New York, NY 10012	Discussion with Black mothers and daughters about menstruation, sexuality, birth control, teenage pregnancy, and relationships.

List of Popular Plays/Books Related to Ethnic Minority Women

Author	Title	Publisher
M. Hong Kingston	The Woman Warrior	Knopf
M. Angelou	I Know Why the Caged Bird Sings	Bantam
A. Walker	The Color Purple	Pocket
C. Niethammer	Daughters of the Earth	Macmillian
N. Shange	For Colored Girls Who Have Considered Suicide When the Rainbow is Enuf	Bantam
A. Flores and K. Flores (Eds.)	The Defiant Muse: Hispanic Feminist Poems	Feminist Press
A. Smedley	Portraits of Chinese Women in Revolution	Feminist Press
B. Paik (Ed.)	Korean American Writings	Insight
I. Stewart	A Voice in Her Tribe: A Woman's Own Story	Ballena
E. Wong Telemaque	It's Crazy to Stay Chinese in Minnesota	Thomas Nelson

Guest Speakers for Presentations in Intracultural and Intercultural Similarities and Distinctiveness

Office of Affirmative Action
Department of Anthropology
United Negro College Fund
Center for Pan African Culture
Foreign Language Department
African American Affairs
Department of History
Latin America Studies Program
International Student Affairs
International and Comparative Programs
Department of Psychology
Women's Studies

Sample Discussion Questions

- We often portray women of Color as a unified group. In fact, each of the women of Color represents a different involvement with the family, labor force, etc. Cite some barriers to the following women: Hispanic, Black, Asian, Native American.

- Discuss some cultural stereotypes concerning women (*e.g.*, their relationship to parents, husband, children). Are they related to legitimate division of labor?

- Why are lesbian and gay relationships considered socially acceptable in some cultures and not in others?

- Pretend you have been asked to design a culture that would ensure equal roles and status for women and men. What aspect(s) of the following cultures would you incorporate in your own: Asian, Hispanic, Black, Native American. Explain the reasons for your choice.

- Describe the ways individuals from other cultures have influenced your own identity.

- In what ways have you learned your values from individuals from various cultures?

- Discuss one of the fundamental problems in research on racial differences: the confounding of race and social class variables.

- Discuss how sex-based labor division patterns in various cultures relate to the status of women and men within the culture.

- Describe ways sexism is not the same for all ethnic and cultural groups.

Exercise: Designing a Sex Fair Culture

Steps for Completing the Exercise:

1. Discuss the rationale behind the radical experiments several "progressive cultures" have attempted with gender roles.

2. Discuss the reasons for why these gender-role experiments probably failed.

3. Arrange the classroom so that the students can form a fishbowl with an outer and an inner group.

4. Ask students in the inner group to design a sex-fair culture today, ensuring equal roles and status for women and men. Have a recorder jot down the points listed. This discussion should take 15–20 minutes.

5. Allow 5–10 minutes at the end for those students in the outer group to make comments.

6. Post the major conclusions that are drawn from the discussion.

7. Have the class discuss the evidence they have for their suggestions.

8. Make the distinction between the terms identical and equal.

Exercise: Representation of Women of Color in the Media

This exercise is adapted from one designed by Darlene C. DeFour. It is used here with her permission.

Steps for Completing the Exercise:

1. Ask students to take notes during the next 4–5 television programs they watch and magazines they read.

2. This notetaking will involve recording the number of women of Color they see on television and in magazines.

3. Ask students to contrast these figures with: (a) the number of White women; (b) the number of White men and; (c) the number of men of Color.

4. Have students record the number of women of Color portrayed as wives, mothers, career-women, all three.

5. Again ask students to contrast these figures with the groups listed above.

6. Post these results.

7. Have the class discuss the interaction of gender role and racial stereotypes.

Exercise: Cultural Milieu

Steps for Completing the Exercise:

1. Ask students to write a short essay about their own cultural milieu. Have students describe the neighborhood in which they grew up. Ask students to describe the values of this cultural milieu in terms of achievement, independence, marriage. Have students describe how these values affected them as they were growing up.

2. Invite students to share their responses with the class.

103

Exercise: Conversation Hour on Cultural Similarities and Distinctiveness

Steps for Completing the Exercise:

1. Ask students to form an inner and outer fishbowl.

2. In the inner fishbowl, ask a group of 4–5 women of Color to discuss issues relating to child rearing, sexuality, employed mothers.

3. Following this discussion (15–20 minutes), ask students in the outer fishbowl to generate themes from the conversation dealing with cultural similarities and distinctiveness.

4. Ask students to discuss what they learned from the conversation hour in terms of stereotypes *vs.* realities of women of Color.

5. Discuss research on the psychology of women of Color. Sample references are presented in this chapter.

Part 3

Life-Span Development Issues

Chapter 4

Life-Span Development and the Psychology of Women

Sample Outline: Life-Span Development and the Psychology of Women

Conception and Pregnancy

Prenatal sexual development
Chromosomal sex
Sex chromosomal abnormalities
Prenatal environmental influences: Impact on mothers
  drugs
  maternal infectuous and noninfectuous diseases
  maternal nutrition
  maternal age and parity
  maternal stress
Natural childbirth
Complications of pregnancy
Caesarian sections
Artificial insemination
Surrogate motherhood
Abortion

Infancy and Childhood

Physiological sex similarities and differences
  male vulnerability
  physical size
  perceptual development

Interpersonal behavior and attachment
  activity level
  dependency
  fear and anxiety
  nurturance
  aggression
  compliance
  dominance
  irritability

intellectual capabilities
stability of gender and sex similarities and differences

Theories of children's acquisition of a gender-role identity
psychoanalytic theory
social learning theory
cognitive-developmental theory
gender schema theory

Adults' responses and interactions with infants
effect of sex label on interactions between infants and adults
distal stimulation
proximal stimulation
toy choices
attributions about personality
knowledge of infant and child development

Peer influences on gender-role development
segregation of sexes
prejudice against opposite sex peers
play
differential expectations

School influences
school structure
behavior of teachers
textbooks
tests
non-sexist school curricula

Media
books
television
rock music videos
music

Adolescence

Physical and health aspects of adolescence
developmental sequence of pubescence in girls
menarche
menstruation
early *vs.* late maturation
development of secondary sex characteristics
eating disorders

Identity/self concept issues
self-conscious behavior
egocentrism

    personal fable
    imaginary audience

Personal choices and social scripts
    sexuality in adolescence
    teenage pregnancy
    sexy *vs.* sexual: double bind for adolescent women
    contraception
    sexually transmitted diseases
    lesbian relationships
    bisexual relationships
    celibacy
    dating
    teenage marriage

Career development
    femininity/achievement incompatibility
    contingency training
    career choice
    nonsexist school curricula
    math anxiety

Adulthood

Stereotypes about older women: Double standard of aging

Changes in aspects of gender role identity in adulthood

Physical aspect of older adulthood
    mastectomy
    hysterectomy
    arthritis
    osteoporosis
    menopause
    health and sex
    health care and older women
    disease-free aging

Achievement/career issues
    multiple careers over the lifespan
    retirement
    leisure
    older women as students

Personal choices and social scripts
    sexuality and the older woman
    motherhood and grandmotherhood
    older lesbian women
    nonmarital heterosexual older women

marriage
empty nest issues
infertility
widowhood
divorce
voluntary childlessness
remarriage
singlehood

Adjustment
life satisfaction
death
psychosocial well-being of older women
living environment and support systems
therapeutic issues for older women

Sample References

Reviews

Baruch, G., and Brooks-Gunn, J. (Eds.) (1984). *Women in Midlife.* New York: Plenum.

Boston Lesbian Psychologies Collective (Eds.) (1987). *Lesbian Psychologies: Explorations and Challenges.* Champaign, IL: University of Illinois Press.

Deaux, K. (1985). "Sex and gender." *Annual Review of Psychology, 36,* 49–81.

Giele, J.A. (Ed.) (1982). *Women in the Middle Years: Current Knowledge and Directions for Research and Policy.* New York: Wiley.

Huston, A.C. (1983). "Sex typing." In E.M. Hetherington (Ed.), *Handbook of Child Psychology, vol. IV.* New York: Wiley.

Jacklin, C.N. (1989). "Female and male: Issues of Gender." *American Psychologist, 44,* 127–133.

Jacklin, C.N., and Maccoby, E.E. (1983). "Issues of gender differentiation." In M.D. Levine, W.B. Carey, A.C. Crocker, and R.T. Gross (Eds.), *Developmental-Behavioral Pediatrics.* Philadelphia: Saunders.

Markson, E.W. (1985). "Sex and gender similarities and differences and the development of the young child." In C. McLoughlin and D.F. Gullo (Eds.) *Young Children in Context.* Springfield, IL: Charles C. Thomas.

Shepard-Look, D.L. (1982). "Sex differentiation and the development of sex roles." In B.B. Wolman (Ed.), *Handbook of Developmental Psychology.* Englewood Cliffs, NJ: Prentice-Hall.

110

Prenatal Development, Infancy, Childhood

Bachtold, L.M. (1984). "Antecedents of caregiver attitudes and social behaviors of Hupa Indian and Anglo-American preschoolers in California." *Child Study Journal, 13,* 217–233.

Cann, A., and Haight, J.M. (1983). "Children's perceptions of relative competition in sex-typed occupations." *Sex Roles, 9,* 767–773.

Downs, A.C. (1983). "Letters to Santa Claus: Elementary school age children's sex-typed toy preferences in a natural setting." *Sex Roles, 9,* 159–163.

McLaughlin, S.D., and Micklin, M. (1983). "The timing of the first birth and changes in personal efficacy." *Journal of Marriage and the Family, 45,* 47–55.

Monroe, R.H., Shimmin, H.S., and Munroe, R.L. (1984). "Gender understanding and sex role preference in four cultures." *Developmental Psychology, 20,* 673–682.

Paludi, M.A. (1981). "Sex role discrimination among girls: Effect on IT Scale for Children scores." *Developmental Psychology, 17,* 851–852.

Paludi, M.A., Geschke, D., Smith, M., and Strayer, L. (1984). "The development of a measure of preschoolers' knowledge of sex-determined role standards." *Child Study Journal, 14,* 171–183.

Romer, N., and Cherry, D. (1980). "Ethnic and social class differences in children's sex-role concepts." *Sex Roles, 6,* 245–263.

White, V.K. (1985). "The experience of pregnancy among Hispanic women." *Dissertation Abstracts International, 47,* (4–B), 1795.

Adolescence

Farmer, H.S. (1983). "Career and homemaking plans for high school youth." *Journal of Counseling Psychology, 30,* 40–45.

Lanier, H.B., and Byrne, J. (1981). "How high school students view women: The relationship between perceived attractiveness, occupation, and education." *Sex Roles, 7,* 145–148.

Schab, F. (1982). "Early adolescence in the south: Attitudes regarding the home and religion." *Adolescence, 17,* 605–612.

Smith, E.J. (1982). "The Black female adolescent: A review of the educational, career, and psychological literature." *Psychology of Women Quarterly, 6,* 261–288.

Middle and Older Adulthood

Dunker, B. (1987). "Aging lesbians: Observations and speculations." In Boston

Lesbian Psychologies Collective (Eds.) *Lesbian Psychologies: Explorations and Challenges.* Champaign, IL: University of Illinois Press.

Hess, B., & Waring, J. (1983). "Family relationships of older women: A women's issue." In E.W. Markson (Ed.), *Older Women: Issues and Prospects.* Lexington, Mass.: Lexington Books.

Lang, A.M., and Brody, E.M. (1983). "Characteristics of middle-aged daughters and help to their elderly mothers." *Journal of Marriage and the Family, 45,* 193–202.

Loewenstein, S.F., Bloch, N.E., Campion, J., Epstein, J.S., Gale, P., and Salvatore, M. (1981). "A study of satisfactions and stresses of single women in midlife." *Sex Roles, 7,* 1127–1141.

Lopata, H.Z. (1981). "Widowhood and husband sanctification." *Journal of Marriage and the Family, 43,* 439–450.

Markson, E.W., and Hess, B.B. (1980). "Older women in the city." *Signs, 5,* 5127–5141.

Myron, M., and Bunch, C. (Eds.) (1975). *Lesbianism and the Women's Movement.* Oakland. Diana Press.

Sontag, S. (1979). "The double standard of aging." In J.H. Williams (Ed.), *Psychology of Women: Selected Readings.* New York: Norton.

Szinovacz, M.E. (Ed.) (1982). *Women's Retirement: Policy Implications of Recent Research.* Beverly Hills, Calif.: Sage.

Vega, W.A., Kolody, B., and Valle, J.R. (1986). "The relationship of marital status, confidant support, and depression among Mexican immigrant women." *Journal of Marriage and the Family, 48,* 597–605.

Parental Influences

Barnett, R.C. (1981). "Parental sex-role attitudes and child-rearing values." *Sex Roles, 7,* 837–846.

Fagot, B. (1985). "A cautionary note: Parents' socialization of boys and girls." *Sex Roles, 12,* 471–476.

Langlois, J.H., and Downs, A.C. (1980). "Mothers, fathers, and peers as socialization agents of sex-typed play behaviors in young children." *Child Development, 51,* 1217–1247.

Lansky, L.M. (1967). "The family structure also affects the role model: Sex role attitudes in parents of preschool children." *Merrill-Palmer Quarterly, 13,* 139–150.

Lauer, J.C., and Lauer, R. (1986). *'Til Death do us Part: How Couples Stay Together.* New York: Haworth.

Paludi, M.A., Geschke, D., Smith, M., and Strayer, L.A. (1984). "The development of a measure of preschoolers' knowledge of sex-determined role standards." *Child Study Journal, 14,* 171–183.

Price-Bonham, S., and Skeen, P.L. (1982). "Black and white fathers' attitudes toward children's sex roles." *Psychological Reports, 50,* 1187–1190.

Peer Influences

Hartup, W.W. (1983). "The peer system." In P. Mussen and E. Hetherington (Eds.), *Handbook of Child Psychology.* New York: Wiley.

Karkau, K. (1973). *Sexism in the Fourth Grade.* Pittsburgh, PA: KNOW, Inc.

Plumb, P., and Cowan, G. (1984). "A developmental study of stereotyping and androgynous activity preferences of tomboys, nontomboys, and males." *Sex Roles, 10,* 703–712.

School Influences

Guttentag, M., and Bray, H. (1976). *Undoing Sex Stereotypes: Research and Resources for Educators.* New York: McGraw-Hill.

Kahn, S.E., and Richardson, A. (1983). "Evaluation on a course in sex roles for secondary school students." *Sex Roles, 9,* 431–440.

Marten, L.A., & Matlin, M.W. (1976). "Does sexism in elementary readers still exist?" *The Reading Teacher, 29,* 764–767.

Saario, T.N., Jacklin, C.N., and Tittle, C.K. (1973). *Sex Role Stereotyping in the Public Schools. Harvard Educational Review, 43,* 386–416.

Sadker, M.P., and Sadker, D.M. (1982). *Sex Equity Handbook for Schools.* New York: Longman.

Serbin, A., and O'Leary, K.D. (1975, December). "How nursery schools teach girls to shut up." *Psychology Today, 9,* 57–58, 102–103.

Media Influences

Ashton, E. (1983). "Measures of play behavior: The influence of sex role stereotyped children's books." *Sex Roles, 9,* 43–47.

Chow, E.N. (1985). "The acculturation experience of Asian American women." In A.G. Sargent (Ed.) *Beyond Sex Roles.* St. Paul, Minn.: West

Courtney, A.E., and Whipple, T.W. (1983). *Sex Stereotyping in Advertising.* Lexington, Mass.: Lexington Books.

Foreit, K.G., Agor, T., Byers, J., Larue, J., Lokey, H., Palazzini, M., Patterson,

M., and Smith, L. (1980). "Sex bias in the newspaper treatment of male-centered and female-centered news stories." *Sex Roles, 6,* 475–480.

Reid, P.T. (1979). "Racial stereotyping on television: A comparison of the behavior of both Black and White television characters." *Journal of Applied Psychology, 64,* 465–571.

Zuckerman, D.M., Singer, D.G., and Singer, J.L. (1980). "Children's television viewing, racial and sex-role attitudes." *Journal of Applied Social Psychology, 10,* 281–294.

Theoretical Perspectives on the Acquisition of a Gender-Role Identity

Gender Schema Theory

Bem, S.L. (1981). "Gender schema theory: A cognitive account of sex typing." *Psychological Review, 88,* 354–364.

Bem, S.L. (1983). "Gender schema theory and its implications for child development: Raising gender-aschematic children in a gender schematic society." *Signs, 8,* 598–616.

Cognitive Developmental Theory

Emmerich, W., Goldman, K.S., Kirsch, B., and Dharabany, R. (1977). "Evidence for a transitional phase in the development of gender constancy." *Child Development, 48,* 930–936.

Kohlberg, L. (1966). "A cognitive-developmental analysis of children's sex-role concepts and attitudes." In E.E. Maccoby (Ed.), *The Development of Sex Differences.* Stanford, Calif.: Stanford University Press.

Thompson, S.K. (1975). "Gender labels and early sex-role development." *Child Development, 46,* 339–347.

Social Learning Theory

Block, J.H. (1978). "Another look at sex differentiation in the socialization behaviors of mothers and fathers." In J.A. Sherman and F.L. Denmark (Eds.), *The Psychology of Women: Future Directions in Research.* New York: Psychological Dimensions.

Mischel, W. (1966). "A social-learning view of sex differences in behavior." In E.E. Maccoby (Ed.), *The Development of Sex Differences.* Stanford, Calif.: Stanford University Press.

Raskin, P.A., and Israel, A.C. (1981). "Sex-role imitation in children: Effects of sex of child, sex of model, and sex-role appropriateness of modeled behavior." *Sex Roles, 7,* 1067–1076.

Psychoanalytic Theory

Freud, S. (1965). *New Introductory Lectures on Psychoanalysis.* New York: Norton (Original work published in 1933).

Effect of Sex Label on Individuals' Knowledge of Infant Development

Condry, J.C., and Condry, S. (1976). "Sex differences: A study of the eye of the beholder." *Child Development, 47,* 812–819.

Delk, J.L., Madden, R.B., Livingston, M., and Ryan, T.T. (1986). "Adult perceptions of the infant as a function of gender labeling and observer gender." *Sex Roles, 15,* 527–534.

Paludi, M.A., and Gullo, D.F. (1986). "Effect of sex labels on adults' knowledge of infant development." *Sex Roles, 16,* 19–30.

Rubin, J.Z., Provenzano, F.J., and Luria, A. (1974). "The eye of the beholder: Parents' views on sex of newborns." *American Journal of Orthopsychiatry, 44,* 512–519.

Rytting, M.B., and Carr, J.P. (1978, May). "The effect of gender information on interaction between infants and adults in a general population." Paper presented at the Annual Meeting of the Midwestern Psychological Association, Chicago, IL.

Seavey, C.A., Katz, P.A., and Zalk, S.R. (1975). "Baby X: The effect of gender labels on adult responses to infants." *Sex Roles, 1,* 103–109.

Will, J.A., Self, P.A., and Datan, N. (1976). "Maternal behavior and perceived sex of infant." *American Journal of Orthopsychiatry, 46,* 135–139.

Journals

Sage: A Scholarly Journal on Black Women

Signs: Journal of Women in Culture and Society

Canadian Woman Studies/les Cahrers de la femme

Iris: A Journal About Women

Journal of Elder Abuse and Neglect

Sex Roles

Research on Aging

Journal of Gay and Lesbian Psychotherapy

Women and Health

Women and Aging

Marriage and Family Review

Journal of Divorce

Developmental Psychology

Human Development

Adolescence

Journal of Black Psychology

Psychology of Women Quarterly

Journal of Cross-Cultural Psychology

Journal of Marriage and the Family

Women and Environment

Journal of Feminist Family Therapy

Journal of Multicultural Counseling and Development

Organizations Concerned with Life-Span Development

Organization	*Address*
Society for Research in Child Development	5801 Ellis Avenue Chicago, IL 60637
Midwestern Society for Research in Life-Span Development	
Southwestern Society for Human Development	Information about these regional organizations may be obtained from the national office.
Southeastern Society for Human Development	
American Psychological Association	1200 17 Street NW Washington, DC 20036
Child and Adolescent Depression and Suicide	Center for Affective Disorders University of Wisconsin 600 Highland Avenue Madison, WI 53793
The American Fertility Foundation	2131 Magnolia Avenue Suite 201 Birmingham, AL 35256
International Symposium on Eating Disorders in Adolescents and Young Adults	Secretariat International Symposium on Eating Disorders P.O. Box 394 Tel Aviv 61003, Israel

Audio-Visual Material: Childhood and Adolescence

Title	Distributor	Description
Girls at 12 (Film)	Education Development 55 Chapel Street Newton, MA 02160	Describes three 12-year old girls, their parents' and teachers' views on adolescence.
The Pinks and the Blues (Video)	Time Life Video P.O. Box 666 Radio City Station New York, NY 10019	Gender role stereotyping and children's acquisition of a gender role identity.
Sex-Role Development (Film)	CRM/McGraw-Hill Films P.O. Box 641 Del Mar, CA 92014	Depicts a family attempting to raise a child in a nonstereotyped manner.
Black Women (Film)	National Educational Television 2715 Packard Road Ann Arbor, MI 48104	
Pregnancy After 35 (Film)	Polymorph Films, Inc. 118 South Street Boston, MA 02111	Discusses physical and psychological issues involved in late parenting.
The Family of Man: Birth (Film)	Time-Life Films 10880 Wilshire Blvd. Los Angeles, CA 90024	Adolescence viewed in a variety of cultures.
Women and Aging (Film)	California State University 600 J Street Sacramento, CA 95819	Double standard of aging for women.
All of Our Lives: Women in Their Later Years (Film)	Filmakers Library 124 E. 40th Street New York, NY 10016	Describes divorced and widowed women in their middle and later years.
Love it Like a Fool (Film)	New Day Films 22 Riverview Drive Wayne, NJ 07470	Features songwriter and folksinger Malvina Reynolds shortly before her death.
Osteoporosis (Video)	Milner-Fenwick 2125 Greenspring Timonium, MD 21093	Description about avoiding and treating osteoporosis.
Maggie Kuhn: Wrinkled Radical (Film)	Indiana University Audio-Visual Center Bloomington, IN 47405	Discussion with the founder of the Grey Panthers.

I Know All Three (Film)	Women Make Movies 225 Lafayette St. New York, NY 10012	Describes Mexican women's friendships.
The Double Day (Film)	Tricontinental Films 333 Avenue of the Americas New York, NY 10014	Discussion of role strain among employed mothers.
Suzanne, Suzanne (Film)	Third World Newsreel 335 W. 38th St. New York, NY 10018	Describes drug abuse, alcoholism, and domestic violence in Black families.
Bottle Babies (Film)	Audio-Visual Room 860 475 Riverside Dr. New York, NY 10115	Discusses the impact of infant formula on women and children in Third World countries.
Daughter Rite (Film)	Iris Films Box 5353 Berkeley, CA 94703	Discussion about mother/daughter and sister/sister relationships.
In the Best Interests of the Children (Film)	Iris Films Box 5353 Berkeley, CA 94703	Lesbian mothers discuss their experiences.
Choosing Children (Film)	Women's Educational Media 175 Duncan St. San Francisco, CA 94110	Discussion about lesbians becoming parents.
It Happens to Us (Film)	New Day Films 22 Riverview Dr. Wayne, NJ 07470	Documentary about abortion.
Pink Triangles (Film)	Cambridge Documentary Films P.O. Box 385 Cambridge, MA 02139	Prejudice against lesbians and gays.
Granny Midwives (Film)	Women Make Movies 325 Lafayette St. New York, NY 10012	Discusses training of granny midwives in Nicaragua.

Popular Books

Title	Author	Publisher
The Woman Warrior	M.H. Kingston	Knopf
The Women's Room	M. French	Jove
Femininity	S. Brownmiller	Simon & Schuster
Outrageous Acts and Everyday Rebellions	G. Steinem	Holt, Rinehart, & Winston
Knock Wood	C. Bergen	Simon & Schuster
The Managerial Woman	M. Hennig and A. Jardim	Doubleday
To be Young, Gifted, and Black	L. Hansberry	Prentice-Hall
A Voice in Her Tribe	I. Stewart	Ballena
Historical, Literary, and Erotic Aspects of Lesbianism	M. Kehoe	Haworth
The Color Purple	A. Walker	Pocket
Portraits of Chinese Women in Revolution	A. Smedley	Feminist Press

Guest Speakers for Presentations on Life-Span Development Issues

Developmental Psychologist

Gerontology Center

Family and Consumer Studies

Personality Psychologist

Communications Specialist

Early Childhood Education

Women's Studies

Teleproductions

Child and Family Therapist

Lesbian and Gay Therapist

Advertising Department

Graphics Production

Continuing Education

Sample Discussion Questions

- Discuss how middle aged and older women have not received adequate attention in research in psychology.

- Describe how women's friendship formation and the establishment of romantic relationships are affected by gender-role stereotypes.

- Discuss how menopause may be used to explain women's psychological reactions in middle adulthood.

- Describe how psychoanalytic theory, social learning theory, cognitive developmental theory, and gender schema theory would explain: (a) five year old Mary playing with a doll; (b) five year old John playing with a doll.

- Adolescent women are especially concerned with how their peers view them. What implication does this have for adolescent women's: (a) receptivity to advertisements on television and in magazines and; (b) willingness to participate in class discussions.

- Discuss several explanations for the development of lesbianism.

- Discuss the convergence of sexism and racism in terms of predicting feminist definitions of lifestyle choices.

- Discuss the way all forms of media convey gender-role stereotypes of girls and women in an exaggerated way.

- Explain why adolescence is the time when the sexes diverge in several areas of cognitive and personality development.

- Briefly discuss the role of teratogens and critical periods in the developing fetus.

- Briefly discuss some ways in which the fetus influences the pregnant woman. Be sure to include physical and social as well as career issues.

- Discuss some gender differences in parent-infant interactions. Be sure to include the following topics: vocalization, handling, knowledge of infant development.

List of Non-Sexist Children's and Adolescents' Stories and Books

For more complete bibliographies, consult:

Adell, J., and Klein, H.D. (1976). *A guide to non-sexist children's books.* Chicago: Academy Press.

Bracken, J., and Wigutoff, S. (1981). *Books for today's young readers: An annotated bibliography of recommended fiction for ages 10–14.* Old Westbury, NY: The Feminist Press.

The following organizations offer a variety of resources on non-sexist childrearing and teaching:

Action for Children's Television
46 Austin St.
Newtonville, MA 02160

American Library Association
Committee on the Status of Women
50 East Huron St.
Chicago, IL 60611

Change for Children
2588 Mission St.
San Francisco, CA 94110

Feminist Press
City University of New York
311 East 94th St.
New York, NY 10128

Lollipop Power
P.O. Box 1171
Chapel Hill, NC 27514

Ms. Magazine
370 Lexington Ave.
New York, NY 10017

National Education Association
1201 Sixteenth St.
Washington, DC 20036

Children's Book Council
175 Fifth Avenue
New York, NY 10010

Public Action Coalition on Toys
38 W. 9th St.
New York, NY 10011

Women on Words and Images
P.O. Box 2163
Princeton, NJ 08540

National Organization for Women
425 13th St. NW
Washington, DC 20004

Preschool Through Third Grade

Father gander nursery rhymes: The equal rights amendment
Douglas Larche
Advocacy
1986

Diana and her rhinoceros
Edward Ardizzone
Walck
1964

Boys and girls, girls and boys
Eve Merriam
Holt, Rinehart, & Winston
1972

Mommies at work
Scholastic Book Services
1971

Womenfolk and fairy tales
Rosemary Minard
Houghton Mifflin
1975

The queen who couldn't bake gingerbread
Dorothy Van Woerkom
Knopf
1975

Ruby!
Amy Aitken
Bradbury
1979

There was nobody there
Barbara Bottner
Macmillian
1978

Amy for short
Laura Joffee Numeroff
Macmillian
1976

Hurray for captain Jane!
Sam Reavin
Parents' Magazine
1971

Hester the jester
   Ben Shecter
   Harper & Row
   1977

My very own special body book
   Kerry Bassett
   Hawthorne
   1980

Let's paint a rainbow
   Eric Carle
   Philomel
   1983

Just us women
   Jeanette Caines
   Harper & Row
   1983

Play it safe: The kids guide to personal safety and crime prevention
   Kathy Kyte
   Knopf
   1983

Red flag green flag people
   Joy Williams
   Rape and Abuse Center
   1980

Fourth Through Seventh Grade

Kick a stone home
   Doris Buchanan Smith
   Crowell
   1974

Nothing is impossible: The story of Beatrix Potter
   Dorothy Aldis
   Atheneum
   1969

I'm nobody, who are you? The story of Emily Dickinson
   Edna Barth
   Seabury
   1971

Women in win
  Francene Sabin
  Random House
  1975

Naomi
  Bernice Rabe
  Nelson
  1975

Girls are equal too
  Dale Carlson
  Atheneum
  1975

Law and the new woman
  Mary McHugh
  Franklin Watts
  1975

The boy who wanted a baby
  Wendy Lichtman
  Feminist Press
  1983

Seafaring women
  Linda Grant DePauw
  Houghton Mifflin
  1983

Embers: Stories for a changing world
  Ruth S. Meyers and Beryle Banfield
  Feminist Press
  1983

Choices: A teen woman's journal for self-awareness and personal
planning
  Mindy Bingha, Judy Edmondson, & Sandy Stryker
  Advocacy
  1984

Exercises

Exercise: Effect of Sex Labels on Knowledge of Infant Development

Steps for Completing the Exercise:

1. Prepare three versions of a brief questionnaire assessing students' knowledge of infant development.
   Source: Granger, C. (1982). "Young adolescents' knowledge of infant abilities." *Dissertation Abstracts International, 43.*

Sample Items:

a) At what age are most babies first able to lift their head from time to time when being held upright?

b) At what age do most babies begin to try to imitate simple words?

c) At what age do most babies begin to look steadily at an object that is in their crib?

d) At what age are most babies first able to help while dressing, but putting their arms in shirt sleeves?

2. Three versions need to be prepared: one with the label "boys," one with "girls," and one with the label absent (*i.e.,* "babies").

3. Distribute one version of the questionnaire to one-third of the students. Students must be unaware of the sex label manipulation.

4. Ask students to indicate their response to each item in months, from 0 to 24.

5. Have students determine the number of months their answers deviated from the normative score.

6. Check for gender differences as well as effects due to experience with children (parenting, babysitting, volunteer work, etc.).

7. Check to see whether there are any differences due to the domain of skills described, *i.e.,* motor, language, cognitive, personal-social.

8. Discuss the research on adults' expectations of infant development.

Source: Paludi, M.A., and Gullo, D.F. (1986). "Effects of sex labels on adults' knowledge of infant development." *Sex Roles, 16*, 19–30.

Exercise: Music Videos and the Portrayal of Women and Men

Steps for Completing the Exercise:

1. Acquaint students with the media's antiwoman messages.
   Source: "Misogyny in rock video." Prepared by Evelina Kane. Available from Women Against Pornography, 358 W. 47 Street, New York, NY 10036.

2. Ask students to watch a television station (*e.g.*, MTV on cable) that depicts rock music videos.

3. Ask students to watch 4–5 videos and complete the Bem Sex Role Inventory for the main male and female characters in each video.

4. Also ask students to complete the Attitudes toward Women Scale for each video based on how they believe the director of the video would answer the items.

5. Ask students to compare their ratings on the Bem Sex Role Inventory and Attitudes toward Women Scale with other class members. Look for gender, racial, and ethnic differences in responses to these items.

6. Ask students to describe whether the videos they watched were violent and/or sexist. Have students discuss how the videos perpetuate gender role stereotypes.

Exercise: Children's Gender Role Preference

Steps for Completing the Exercise:

1. Describe the developmental process of children's acquisition of a gender role identity. Distinguish among the following components of a gender role identity:
   preference
   adoption
   identification
   orientation
   knowledge of sex-determined role standards
   Source: Paludi, M.A., Geschke, D., Smith, M., and Strayer, L.A. (1984). "The development of a measure of preschoolers' knowledge of sex-determined role standards." *Child Study Journal, 14*, 171–183.

2. Prepare copies of toys and activities taken from magazines or books.

3. Ask each group to interview four children aged 3–7 years (two girls and two boys).

4. Students are to show each child the pictures one at a time and ask children whether or not they would play with the toy or participate in the activity. For example:
   I am going to show you pictures of things children play with, things children do, and things children want to do when they play grown-ups. I will show you some pictures. When I show you a picture, I want you to tell me if you would like to play with it or do it.

5. Students should record each child's responses.

6. Have students determine whether there are any gender and/or age differences in children's selection of toys and activities.

7. Determine whether there are any sex of experimenter effects.

8. Discuss the class' findings with previous research.
   Source: Sidorowicz, L.S., and Lunney, G.S. (1980). "Baby X revisited." *Sex Roles, 6*, 67–73.
   Kutner, N.G., and Levinson, R.M. (1978). "The toy salesperson: A voice for change in sex-role stereotypes?" *Sex Roles, 4*, 1–7.

9. Ask students to consider the implication of toy choices and play for excellence in spatial ability. Discuss the research on identifying factors that are related to gender differences in spatial ability.
   Source: Nash, S.C. (1975). "The relationship among sex-role stereotyping, Sex-role preference, and sex differences in spatial visualization." *Sex Roles, 1*, 15–32.
   Stericker, A., and LeVesconte, S. (1982). "Effect of brief training on sex-related differences in visual-spatial skill." *Journal of Personality and Social Psychology, 43*, 1018–1029.

Exercise: Character Analysis

Steps for Completing the Exercise:

1. Ask students to select a female character from a play, movie, television program, novel, etc. Some sample selections:
   All in the Family
   Desert Heart
   Crimes of the Heart

Hannah and her Sisters
Woman Warrior
Tootsie
West Side Story
The Women's Room
The Color Purple

2. Ask students to describe the women's gender-role identity in terms of the following areas:
sexuality
relationships with women and men
education
adjustment
achievement

3. Students should write a 5–10 page paper for this character analysis.

4. Set up a mock conference, "The psychology of women through literature and film" at which students can discuss their analysis.

Part 4

Women's Health Issues

Chapter 5

Women and Health

Sample Outline

  menarche

  menstruation

  menstrual taboos and myths

  sources of information about menstruation

  attitudes toward menstruation

  biological aspects of menstruation

  psychological and physical aspects of menstruation

  dysmenorrhea

  amenorrhea

  premenstrual syndrome

  mood swings

  reactions to premenstrual and menstrual women

  menopause

  climacteric

  physical and psychological reactions to menopause

  reactions to menopausal and post-menopausal women

  mastectomy

  osteoporosis

  oophorectomy and hysterectomy

  breast disorders

  DES

  AIDS

disabled women

stress

drugs

women and exercise

nutritional information

Sample References

Images of Women from the Medical Care System

Adelman, S. (1982). "The female surgeon." In J.P. Collan (Ed.), *The Physician: A Professional Under Stress.* (pp. 279–293). Norwalk, Conn.: Appleton-Century-Crofts.

Bluestone, N.R. (1978). "The future impact of women physicians on American medicine." *American Journal of Public Health, 68,* 760–763.

Brown, S.L., and Klein, R.H. (1982). "Women-power in the medical hierarchy." *Journal of the American Medical Women's Association, 37,* 153–164.

Corea, G. (1977). *The Hidden Malpractice: How American Medicine Treats Women as Patients and Professionals.* Garden City, New York: Anchor Press.

Ehrenreich, B., and English, D. (1973). *Complaints and Disorders: The Sexual Politics of Sickness.* Old Westbury, NY: The Feminist Press.

Ehrenreich, B., and English, D. (1973). *For Her Own Good: 150 Years of the Experts' Advice to Women.* Garden City, NJ: Doubleday.

Fee, E. (Ed.) (1983). *Women and Health: The Politics of Sex in Medicine.* New York: Baywood Publishing Co., Inc.

Fidell, L.S. (1980). "Sex role stereotypes and the American physician." *Psychology of Women Quarterly, 4,* 313–330.

Heins, M. (1983). "Update: Women in medicine." *Journal of the American Medical Women's Association, 40,* 43–50.

Leavitt, J. (1984). *Women and Health in America.* Madison, Wis.: University of Wisconsin Press.

Marieskind, H. (1980). *Women in the Health Care System: Patients, Providers, and Programs.* St. Louis, Mis.: C.V. Mosby.

Mendelsohn, R.S. (1982). *Male Practice: How Doctors Manipulate Women.* Chicago: Contemporary Books, Inc.

Roeske, N.C.A. (1983). "Women's studies in medical education." *Journal of Medical Education, 58,* 611–618.

Scully, D. (1980). *Men who Control Women's Health: The Miseducation of Obstetrician-Gynecologists.* Boston: Houghton Mifflin.

General

Bain, L. (1986, November). "Issues of gender, race, and class in health promotion programs." Paper presented at the Annual Conference of Research on Women and Education, Washington, DC.

Blechman, E. and Brownell, K. (Eds.). (1988). *Handbook of Behavioral Medicine for Women.* Elmsford, NY: Pergamon.

Bermosk, L.S., and Porter, S.E. (1979). *Women's Health and Human Wholeness.* New York: Appleton-Century-Crofts.

Golub, S., and Freedman, R.J. (Eds.) (1985). *Health Needs of Women as They Age.* New York: Harrington Park Press.

Grady, K.E., and Lemkau, J.P. (Eds.). (1988). Special Issue: Women's health: our minds, our bodies. *Psychology of Women Quarterly, 12,* (4).

Kannell, W.B., and Brand, F.N. (1983). "Cardio-vascular risk factors in the elderly woman." In E.W. Markson (Ed.), *Older Women* (pp. 315–327). Lexington, Mass.: Lexington Books.

Levy, S.M. (1980–1981). The adjustment of the older woman: Effects of chronic ill health and attitudes toward retirement." *International Journal of Aging and Human Development, 12,* 93–100.

Smith, E.D. (1981). *Women's Healthcare: A Guide for Patient Education.* New York: Appleton-Century-Crofts.

Strickland, B. (1989). "Sex-related differences in health and illness." *Psychology of Women Quarterly, 12,* 381–399.

Warren, M.P. (1983). "Physical and biological aspects of puberty." In J. Brooks-Gunn and A.C. Petersen (Eds.), *Girls at Puberty* (pp. 3–28). New York: Plenum.

Weiss, K. (Ed.) (1984). *Women's healthcare: A Guide to Alternatives.* Reston, VA.: Reston Publishing Co.

DES

Saber, F. (1977). "The DES problem: Fashioning a physician's duty to warn." *Journal of Legal Medicine,* 25–30.

Schwartz, R.W. (1977). "Psychological effects of diethylstilbestrol exposure." *Journal of the American Medical Association, 237,* 252–254.

Disabled Women

Browne, S.E., Connor, P., and Stern, N. (1985). *With the Power of Each Breath: A Disabled Woman's Anthology.* Pittsburgh, Pa.: Cleis Press.

Bullard, D., and Knight, S. (Eds.) (1981). *Sexuality and Physical Disability: Personal Perspectives.* New York: C.V. Mosby.

Fine, M., and Asch, A. (1988). Disability beyond stigma: Social interaction, discrimination, and activism. *Journal of Social Issues, 44,* 3–21.

Osteoporosis

Kerzner, L.J. (1983). "Physical changes after menopause." In E.W. Markson (Ed.), *Older Women* (pp. 299–313). Lexington, Mass.: Lexington Books.

Oophorectomy and Hysterectomy

Ananth, J. (1978). "Hysterectomy and depression." *Obstetrics and Gynecology, 52,* 724.

Budd, H. (1977). "Variations of response to hysterectomy: Bases for individualized care to women." In N. Lytle (Ed.), *Nursing of Women in the Age of Liberation.* Dubuque, IA.: William C. Brown.

Centers for Disease Control (1980). "Surgical sterilization surveillance: Hysterectomy in women aged 15–44, 1970–1975."

Epstein, S. (1979). *The Politics of Cancer.* New York: Anchor Books.

Hunter, D.S. (1976). "Oophorectomy and the surgical menopause." In R.J. Beard (Ed.), *The Menopause* (pp. 212–213). Baltimore: University Park Press.

Breast Disorders and Mastectomy

Grady, K.E. (1988). "Older women and the practice of breast self-examination." *Psychology of Women Quarterly, 12,* 473–487.

Jamison, K.R., Wellisch, D.K., and Pasnau, R.P. (1978). "Psychosocial aspects of mastectomy: I The woman's perspective." *American Journal of Psychiatry, 135,* 432–436.

Kushner, R. (1985). *Alternatives: New Developments in the War on Breast Cancer.* New York: Warner Books.

Love, S. (1982). "Fibrocystic 'disease' of the breast—a nondisease." *New England Journal of Medicine, 307,* 1010–1014.

Meyerowitz, B.E. (1981). "The impact of mastectomy on the lives of women." *Professional Psychology, 12,* 119–127.

Notman, M.T. (1978). "A psychological consideration of mastectomy." In M.T. Notman and C.C. Nadelson (Eds.), *The Woman Patient: Vol. 1. Sexual and Reproductive Aspects of Women's Health Care* ((pp. 247–355). New York: Plenum.

Polivy, J. (1977). "Psychological effects of mastectomy on a woman's feminine self-concept." *Journal of Nervous and mental Disease, 164,* 77–82.

Tishler, S.L. (1978). "Breast disorders." In M.T. Notman and C.C. Nadelson (Eds.), *The Woman Patient. Vol.1: Sexual and Reproductive Aspects of Women's Health Care* (pp. 233–246). New York: Plenum.

Woods, N.F., and Earp, J.L. (1978). "Women with cured breast cancer: A study of mastectomy patients in North Carolina." *Nursing Research, 27,* 279–285.

Menopause

Cowan, G., Warren, L.W., and Young, J.L. (1985). "Medical perceptions of menopausal symptoms." *Psychology of Women Quarterly, 9,* 3–14.

Friederich, M.A. (1982). "Aging, menopause, and estrogens: The clinician's dilemma." In A.M. Voda, M. Dinnerstein, and S.P. O'Donnell (Eds.), *Changing Perspectives on Menopause* (pp. 335–345). Austin, Tx.: University of Texas press.

Goodman, J.J. (1980). "Toward a biology of menopause." *Signs, 5,* 739–753.

Kerzner, L.J. (1983). "Physical changes after menopause." In E.W. Markson (Ed.), *Older Women* (pp. 299–313). Lexington, Mass.: Lexington Books.

Morokoff, P. (1988). "Sexuality in perimenopausal and postmenopausal women." *Psychology of Women Quarterly, 12,* 489–511.

Posner, J. (1979). "It's all in your head: Feminist and medical models of menopause (strange bedfellows)." *Sex Roles, 5,* 179–190.

Woods, N.F. (1982). "Menopausal distress: A model for epidemiologic investigation." In A.M. Voda, M. Dinnerstein, and S.R. O'Donnell (Eds.), *Changing Perspectives on Menopause* (pp. 160–169). Austin, Tx.: University of Texas Press.

Menstruation

Abplanalp, J.M. (1983). "Premenstrual syndrome: A selective review." In S. Golub (Ed.), *Lifting the Curse of Menstruation* (pp. 107–123). New York: Haworth.

Brooks-Gunn, J., and Ruble, D.N. (1983). "The experience of menarche from a developmental perspective." In J. Brooks-Gunn and A.C. Petersen (Eds.), *Girls at Puberty* (pp. 153–177). New York: Plenum.

Fuchs, F. (1980). "Dysmenorrhea and dyspareunia." In R.C. Friedman (Ed.), *Behavior and the Menstrual Cycle* (PP. 199–216). New York: Marcel Bekker.

Golub, S. (Ed.) (1983). *Menarche.* Lexington, Mass.: Lexington Books.

Golub, S. (Ed.) (1983). *Lifting the Curse of Menstruation: A Feminist Appraisal of the Influence of Menstruation on Women's Lives.* New York: Haworth.

Kerzner, L.J. (1983). "Physical changes after menopause." In E.W. Markson (Ed.), *Older Women* (pp. 299–313). Lexington, Mass.: Lexington Books.

Koeske, R. (1980). "Theoretical perspectives on menstrual cycle research: The relevance of attributional approaches for the perception and explanation of premenstrual emotionality." In A.J. Dan, E.A. Graham, and C.P. Bcedher (Eds.), *The Menstrual Cycle, Vol. 1* (pp. 8–25). New York: Springer.

Koff, E. (1983). "Through the looking glass of menarche: What the adolescent girl sees." In S. Golub (Ed.), *Menarche* (pp. 77–86). Lexington, Mass.: Lexington Books.

Laws, S. (1983). "The sexual politics of premenstrual tension." *Women's Studies International Forum, 6,* 19–31.

Milow, V.J. (1983). "Menstrual education: Past, present, and future." In S. Golub (Ed.), *Menarche* (pp. 127–132). Lexington, Mass.: Lexington Books.

Parlee, M.B. (1973). "The premenstrual syndrome." *Psychological Bulletin, 80,* 454–465.

Parlee, M.B. (1983). "Menstrual rhythms in sensory processes: A review of fluctuations in vision, olfaction, audition, taste, and touch." *Psychological Bulletin, 93,* 539–548.

Rierdan, J., and Koff, E. (1980). "The psychological impact of menarche: Integrative versus descriptive changes." *Journal of Youth and Adolescence, 9,* 49–58.

Sommer, B. (1983). "How does menstruation affect cognitive competence and psychophysiological response?" In S. Golub (Ed.), *Lifting the Curse of Menstruation* (pp. 53–90). New York: Haworth.

Stubbs, M., Rierdan, J., and Koff, E. (1986, November). "Becoming a woman: Educating young adolescents about menstruation." Paper presented at the Annual Conference on Research on Women and Education, Washington, DC.

AIDS

Amaro, H. (1988). "Considerations for prevention of HIV infection among Hispanic women." *Psychology of Women Quarterly, 12,* 429–443.

Centers for Disease Control (1988, July 18). *AIDS Weekly Surveillance Report US.* AIDS Program, Atlanta, GA: Author.

DiClemente, R.J., Boyer, C.B., and Morales, E.S. (1988). "Minorities and AIDS: Knowledge, Attitudes, and Misconceptions among Black and Latino Adolescents." *American Journal of Public Health, 78,* 55–57.

Guinan, M.E., and Hardy, A. (1987). "Epidemiology of AIDS in Women in the United States 1981 through 1986." *Journal of the American Medical Association, 257,* 2039–2042.

Shaw, N., and Paleo, L. (1986). "Women and AIDS." In L. McKusick (Ed.), *What to do about AIDS: Physicians and Mental Health Professionals Discuss the Issues.* Los Angeles: University of California Press.

Pamphlets, Brochures, Symposia, and Periodicals

Broomstick (A newsletter by, for, and about women over forty)
Options for Women over Forty
3543 18 Street
San Francisco, CO 94110

Hot Flash (A newsletter for midlife and older women)
School of Allied Health Professionals
State University of New York
Health Sciences Center
Stony Brook, NY 11794

Medical Self-Care Magazine
P.O. Box 718
Inverness, Ca 94937

Cowan, B. (1977). *Women's Health Care: Resources, Writings, Bibliographies.* Ann Arbor, MI: Anshen Publications.

Belden, N. "The plight of the DES daughter: Suggestions for government action. Diethylstibestrol (DES), a health resource guide, Number 6." Available from National Women's Health Network, 2025 Eye Street, N.W., Suite 105, Washington, DC 20006.

Coalition of the Medical Rights of Women. *D.E.S.* CMRW, 4079 A 24 Street, San Francisco, CA 94114.

Morgan, S. (1978). *Hysterectomy.* Available from the author, 2921 Walnut Avenue, Manhatten Beach, CA 90266.

The following companies produce media material explaining the menstrual cycle:

Kimberly-Clark Corporation
Newark International Plaza
Newark, NJ

National Women's Health Network
1302 18 Street
Washington, DC 20036

Tampax Incorporated
Educational Department
5 Dakota Drive
Lake Success, NY

Organizations Concerned with Women and Health

Organization	Address
American Cancer Society	777 Third Avenue New York, NY 10017
Breast Cancer Advisory Center	Box 224 Kensington, MD 20895
Food and Drug Administration	5600 Fishers Lane Rockville, MD 20852
Black Women's Health Project	Martin Luther King Community Center Suite 157 450 Auburn Avenue, NE Atlanta, GA 30312
Boston Self-Help Center	18 Williston Rd. Brookline, MA 02146
Cassandra: Radical Feminist Nurses Network	P.O. Box 341 Williamsville, NY 14221
Coalition for the Medical Rights of Women	Box 10426 Oakland, CA 94610
Massachusetts Institute of behavioral Medicine	1145 Main Street Suite 416 Springfield, MA 01103
DES Action	2845 24 Street San Francisco, CA 94117
Hysterectomy Educational Resources and Services	501 Woodbrook Avenue Philadelphia, PA 19119

Committee for Freedom of Choice in Cancer Therapy	146 Main Street Suite 408 Los Altos, CA 94022
Endometriosis Association	238 West Wisconsin Avenue Milwaukee, WI 53202
Feminist Women's Health Center	6411 Hollywood Blvd. Los Angeles, CA 90028
Gay Nurses Alliance	44 St. Mark's Place New York, NY 10003
Institute for the Study of Medical Ethics	P.O. Box 17307 Los Angeles, CA 90017
New Hampshire Feminist Health Center	38 South Main Street Concord, NH 03301
Women Healthsharing	Box 230 Station M Toronto, Ontario M6S 4T3
Elderhostel	100 Boylston Street Suite 200 Boston, MA 02116
National Hospice Organization	1311-A Dolly Madison Blvd. McLean, VA 22101
SHARE	Self-Help Action Rap Experience 34 Gramercy Park New York, NY 10003
Arthritis Information Clearing House	P.O. Box 34427 Bethesda, MD 20034
Project on the Handicapped in Science	American Association of Science 1776 Massachusetts Ave., NW Washington, DC 20036
Environmental Protection Agency	Public Information Center 401 M Street, NW Washington, DC 20460
American Medical Women's Association	465 Grand Street New York, NY 10002
American Lung Association	Box 596-MS New York, NY 10001
American Health and Diet Company	475 Park Avenue South New York, NY 10016
Asian Women's Health Project	University of California Los Angeles, CA 90024

Audio-Visual Material

Title	Distributor	Description
Taking Our Bodies Back: The Women's Health Movement (Film)	Cambridge Documentary Films P.O. Box 385 Cambridge, MA 02139	Demonstrates the use of a speculum and discusses natural childbirth, hysterectomy, and obtaining health care.
The Family of Man: Teenagers (Film)	Time-Life Films 10880 Wilshire Blvd. 17th Floor Los Angeles, CA 90024	Documents how women from a variety of cultures experience menarche.
Dear Diary (Film)	New Day Films 22 Riverview Drive Wayne, NJ 07470	Discusses body self-image and peer pressure.
Breast Self-Examination (Video)	Milner-Fenwick 2125 Greenspring Drive Timonium, MD 21093	Describes self-examination and breast disorders.
Osteoporosis (Video)	Milner-Fenwick 2125 Greenspring Drive Timonium, MD 21093	Discusses osteoporosis, how to avoid it, and how to help it.

Popular Books

Title	Author/Editor	Publisher
General		
The A to Z of Women's Health: A Concise Encyclopedia	C. Ammer	Everest House
Womancare: A Gynecological Guide to Your Body	L. Madaras and J. Patterson	Avon
Maggie's Woman Book	M. Lettvin	Houghton-Mifflin
New Our Bodies, Ourselves	Boston Women's Health Collective	Simon & Schuster
Politics of Women's Health Care		
The Hidden Malpractice: How American Medicine Mistreats Women	G. Corea	Morrow
The American Health Empire: Power, Profits, and Politics	B. Ehrenreich and J. Ehrenreich	Random House

DES: The Complete Story	C. Orenberg	St. Martin's Press
Endometriosis		
Womancare	L. Madaras and J. Patterson	Avon
A Woman; Guide to Endometriosis	J. Older	Schribner
Osteoporosis		
Stand Tall! The Informed Woman's Guide to Osteoporosis	M. Notelovitz and M. Ware	Triad
Menopause		
Menopause: A Positive Approach	R. Reitz	Penguin
The Menopause Book	L. Rose	Hawthorn
Menopause: A Self-Care Manual	Santa Fe Health Education Project	
The Women's Health Movement: Feminist Alternatives to Medical Control	S. Ruzek	Praeger
Men who Control Women's Health: The Miseducation of Obstetrician-Gynecologists	D. Scully	Houghton-Mifflin
Cancer		
Cancer Survivors and How They Did it	J. Glassman	Dial Press
First you Cry	B. Rollin	Lippincott
Hysterectomy		
Coping with Hysterectomy	S. Morgan	Dial Press
Menstruation		
The Curse: A Cultural History of Menstruation	J. Delany, M.J. Lupton, and E. Toth	Dutton
DES		
DES Daughter	J. Bichler	Avon
DES: The Bitter Pill	R. Meyers	Putnam

Guest Speakers for Presentations on Women and Health

School of Nursing

Public Health Nurse

Department of Behavioral Medicine/Health Psychology

Department of Psychology

Rehabilitation Counseling

Health Science Center

AIDS counselor

Registered Nurses Association

School Health Association

Medical School/Hospitals

American Cancer Society

Sports Medicine Department

Exercise Physiology

Lesbian Women's and Gay Men's Alliance

Gynecologist

Gynecological Surgeon

Rheumatologist

Sample Discussion Questions

- Describe why women's menstrual periods were used as a reason to keep women away from pursuing their educational and career goals.

- Discuss the research concerning mood swings and performance during the menstrual cycle.

- Describe the psychological reactions to menopause.

- Discuss how the perception of a body change is magnified by cultural factors.

- What evidence do you have that women are taking control over their own health?

- Discuss the controversies surrounding menopausal women taking estrogen.

- Discuss feminist physicians' approach to women's health.

- What recommendations can you make for women learning more about their physical health?

- Design an educational curriculum for junior high and senior high school women about menarche.

Exercises

Exercise: Health Problems of Women

Steps for Completing the Exercise:

1. Ask students to indicate the major health problems they believe women face today.

2. Post these responses on the board; have students self-select into groups who want to investigate one of the problems in more depth.

3. Ask students to have their group find out the most recent feminist research dealing with the health problem.

4. Have students report to the entire class the summary of their findings.

5. Prepare for the class a list of references for each health problem discussed.

6. Invite a speaker (see sample list provided) to discuss women's centers and/or groups that deal with these problems.

7. Ask students to discuss any signs of change they believe suggests more women are taking control over their own health.

8. Provide students with a list of agencies and organizations concerned with women's health problems (See sample list provided).

Exercise: Telling Adolescent Women about Menarche

Steps for Completing the Exercise:

1. Have the students in the class break up into pairs.

2. Ask one student of each pair to pretend she/he is caretaker of the other student.

3. Ask the "caretakers" to have a talk with their "adolescent" about menarche, both physical and psychological issues.

4. Allow 15–20 minutes for these discussions.

5. Ask participants to discuss their performance in this exercise. Deal with

the following issues: embarrassment, controversial issues discussed or ignored, whether accurate information was provided.

6. Provide students with information about popular books on menarche and menstruation.

Exercise: Premenstrual Phase and Coping

This exercise is adapted from M. Matlin (1987) and is used here with permission from Holt, Rinehart, and Winston Publishers.

Steps for Completing the Exercise:

1. Ask students to form groups of four or five.

2. Prepare a handout containing the questions listed below. Ask students to answer these questions aloud for their group. Men in the groups may be asked to answer the questions for a woman they know.

3. Discuss the students' answers with the entire class. Post major conclusions on the board.

4. Note any gender similarities and differences as well as racial, ethnic, age, and SES factors.

5. Discuss men's cycles and mood fluctuations.
   Source: Ramey, E. (1972). "Men's cycles." *Ms.*, Spring, 8–14.

6. Provide students with information about coping with the premenstrual syndrome.
   Source: Abplanalp, J.M. (1983). "Premenstrual syndrome: A selective review." In S. Golub (Ed.), *Lifting the curse of menstruation* (pp. 107–123). New York: Haworth.
   Milow, V.J. (1983). "Menstrual education: Past, present, and future." In S. Golub (Ed.), *Menarche* (pp. 127–132). Lexington, Mass.: Lexington Books.

Questions:

1. Do you experiences any changes in your mood before menstruation?

2. Do you find that you can function as well in your studies when it is several days before your period, in comparison to the rest of your cycle?

3. Do you make any special changes in your diet when you are in your premenstrual phase?

4. Have you heard of "premenstrual syndrome," which refers to the variety of symptoms that can occur before menstruation?

5. Do you experience any of the following during the premenstrual phase: headaches, tenderness of the breasts, swelling, or acne?

6. What activities do you believe women who experience premenstrual syndrome should participate in?

7. Are you aware of the controversy surrounding the use of medication for premenstrual syndrome?

Exercise: Personal Health Care

Steps for Completing the Exercise:

1. Ask students to find out about health problems women in their families have faced.

2. Ask students to determine some precursors of health at midlife, *e.g.,* how nutrition, vitamins, and exercise affect osteoporosis, diabetes, etc.

3. Have students locate supportive environments for women with the health problems they have listed, *e.g.,* self-help groups, women's health centers, etc.

4. Invite women from these centers to talk to the class so women can learn about health through sharing and validating their experiences with each other.

5. Discussions focusing on the information presented in the *New Our Bodies, Ourselves* would prove informative and empowering.

Chapter 6

Adjustment and Psychotherapy

Sample Outline

Women as providers in the mental health care system

Female *vs.* male therapists: Does it make a difference?

Sample References

Gender and problems of Adjustment

Al-Issa, I. (1982). "Gender and adult psychopathology." In I. Al-Issa (Ed.), *Gender and Psychopathology.* New York: Academic Press.

Atkinson, A.K., and Rickel, A.U. (1984). "Depression in women: The postpartum experience." In A.U. Rickel, M. Gerrard, and I. Iscoe (Eds.), *Social and Psychological Problems of Women: Prevention and Crisis Intervention.* New York: Hemisphere.

Belle, D. (1984). "Inequality and mental health: Low income and minority women." In L.E. Walker (Ed.), *Women and Mental Health Policy.* Beverly Hills, Cal.: Sage.

Boskind-Lodahl, M. (1976). "Cinderella's stepsisters: A feminist perspective on anorexia nervosa and bulimia." *Signs, 2,* 120–146.

Canino, G. (1982). "The Hispanic woman: Sociocultural influences on diagnoses and treatment." In R.M. Becerra, M. Karno, and J. Escobar (Eds.), *The Hispanic Mental Health: Latina Women in Transition.* New York: Hispanic Research Center.

Caplan, P.J. (1985). *The Myth of Women's Masochism.* New York: E.P. Dutton.

Chesler, P. (1972). *Women and Madness.* Garden City: Doubleday.

Davidson, C., and Abramowitz, S. (1980). "Women as patients." *Psychology of Women Quarterly, 4,* 309–423.

Gatz, M., Pearson, C., and Fuentes, M. (1984). "Older women and mental health." In A.U. Rickel, M. Gerrard, and I. Iscoe (Eds.), *Social and Psychological Problems of Women: Prevention and Crisis Intervention.* New York: Hemisphere.

Gomberg, E., and Franks, V. (1979). *Gender and Disordered Behavior.* New York: Brunner/Mazel.

Gove, W.R., and Tudor, J.F. (1973). "Adult sex roles and mental illness." *American Journal of Sociology, 78,* 812–835.

Horowitz, A.V. (1982). "Sex-role expectations, power, and psychological distress." *Sex Roles, 8,* 607–624.

Mulvey, A., and Dohrenwend, B.S. (1984). "The relation of stressful life events to gender." In A.U. Rickel, M. Gerrard, and I. Iscoe (Eds.), *Social and*

Psychological Problems of Women: Prevention and Crisis Intervention. New York: Hemisphere.

Radloff, L. (1975). "Sex differences in depression: The effects of occupation and marital status." *Sex Roles, 1,* 249–265.

Rodin, J., Silberstein, L., and Striegel-Moore, R. (1985). "Women and weight: A normative discontent." In T. B. Sonderegger (Ed.), *Nebraska Symposium on Motivation, 1984: Psychology and Gender.* Lincoln, Neb.: University of Nebraska Press.

Schlesier-Stropp, B. (1984). "Bulimia: A review of the literature." *Psychological Bulletin, 95,* 247–257.

Wooley, S., and Wooley, O.W. (1980). "Eating disorders: Obesity and anorexia." In A. Brodsky and R. Hare-Mustin (Eds.), *Women and Psychotherapy.* New York: Guilford.

Sexism and Psychotherapy

Abramowitz, S.I. (1976). "Sex bias in psychotherapy: A failure to confirm." *American Journal of Psychiatry, 133,* 706–709.

American Psychological Association. (1975). "Report of the task force on sex bias and sex-role stereotyping in psychotherapeutic practice." *American Psychologist, 30,* 1169–1175.

American Psychological Association. (1978). "Task force on sex bias and sex-role stereotyping in psychotherapeutic practice. Source materials for non-sexist therapy." *JSAS Catalog of Selected Documents in Psychology* (Ms. 1685).

Broverman, I.K., Broverman, D.M., Clarkson, F.E., Rosenkrantz, P.S., and Vogel, S.R. (1970). "Sex role stereotypes and clinical judgments of mental health." *Journal of Consulting and Clinical Psychology, 34,* 1–7.

Buczek, T.A. (1981). "Sex bias in counseling: Counselor retention of the concerns of a female and male client." *Journal of Counseling Psychology, 28,* 13–21.

Carmen, E., Russo, N., and Miller, J. (1981). "Inequality and women's mental health: An overview." *American Journal of Psychiatry, 138,* 1319–1330.

Gomes, B., and Abramowitz, S.I. (1976). "Sex-related patient and therapist effects on clinical judgment." *Sex Roles, 2,* 1–14.

Hare-Mustin, R.T. (1983). "An appraisal of the relationship between women and psychotherapy: 80 years after the case of Dora." *American Psychologist, 38,* 593–601.

Holroyd, J.C., and Brodsky, A.M. (1977). "Psychologists' attitudes and practices regarding erotic and nonerotic physical contact with patients." *American Psychologist, 34,* 843–849.

Kaplan, M. (1983). "A woman's view of DSM-III." *American Psychologist, 38,* 786–792.

Maracek, J., and Johnson, M. (1980). "Gender and the process of therapy." In A.M. Brodsky and R.T. Hare-Mustin (Eds.), *Women and Psychotherapy* (pp. 67–93). New York: Guilford.

Masson, J.M. (1984, February). "Freud and the seduction theory." *Atlantic Monthly,* 33–60.

Shapiro, J. (1977). "Socialization of sex roles in the counseling setting: Differential counselor behavioral and attitudinal responses to typical and atypical female sex roles." *Sex Roles, 3,* 173–184.

Sherman, J.A. (1980). "Therapist attitudes and sex-role stereotyping." In A.M. Brodsky and R.T. Hare-Mustin (Eds.), *Women and Psychotherapy.* New York: Guilford.

Smith, M. (1980). Sex bias in counseling and psychotherapy. *Psychological Bulletin, 87,* 392–407.

Alternatives to Traditional Psychotherapy

Brodsky, A. (1977). "Therapeutic aspects of consciousness-raising groups." In E.I. Rawlings and D.K. Carter (Eds.), *Psychotherapy for Women.* Springfield, IL: Charles C. Thomas.

Brodsky, A.M. (1980). "A decade of feminist influence on psychotherapy." *Psychology of Women Quarterly, 4,* 331–344.

Brodsky, A.M., and Hare-Mustin, R.T. (Eds.) (1980). *Women and Psychotherapy.* New York: Guilford.

Brown, L. (1987). "Lesbians, weight, and eating: New analyses and perspectives." In Boston Lesbian Psychologies Collective (Eds.), *Lesbian Psychologies: Explorations and Challenges.* Urbana, IL: University of Illinois Press.

Gilbert, L.A. (1980). "Feminist therapy." In A. Brodsky and R.T. Hare-Mustin (Eds.), *Women and Psychotherapy.* New York: Guilford.

Hare-Mustin, R.T. (1983). "An appraisal of the relationship between women and psychotherapy." *American Psychologist, 38,* 593–601.

Holyroyd, J.C., and Brodsky, A.M. (1977). "Psychologists' attitudes and practices regarding erotic and nonerotic physical contact with patients." *American Psychologist, 32,* 843–849.

Kaplan, A.G. (1976). "Androgyny as a model of mental health for women: From theory to therapy." In A.G. Kaplan and J.P. Bean (Eds.). *Beyond Sex-Role Stereotypes: Readings Toward a Psychology of Androgyny.* Boston, Mass.: Little, Brown.

Kaplan, A.G. (1979). "Clarifying the concept of androgyny: Implications for therapy." *Psychology of Women Quarterly, 3,* 223–230.

Howard, D. (Ed.) (1987). *A Guide to Dynamics of Feminist Therapy.* New York: Haworth.

Kirsh, B. (1974). "Consciousness-raising groups as therapy for women." In V. Franks and V. Burtle (Eds.), *Women in Therapy.* New York: Brunner/Mazel.

Kravetz, D. (1980). "Consciousness-raising and self-help." In A. Brodsky and R. Hare-Mustin (Eds.), *Women and Psychotherapy.* New York: Guilford.

Lorion, R.P., & Broughan, K.G. (1984). "Differential needs and treatment approaches for women in psychotherapy." In A.U. Rickel, M. Gerrard, and I. Iscoe (Eds.), *Social and Psychological Problems of Women: Prevention and Crisis Intervention.* New York: Hemisphere.

Mowbray, C., Lanir, S., and Hulce, M. (Eds.). (1984). *Women and Mental Health: New Directions for Change.* New York: Haworth Press.

Rawlings, E.I., and Carter, D.K. (Eds.). (1977). *Psychotherapy for Women: Treatment Toward Equality.* Springfield, IL: Charles C. Thomas.

Robbins, J., and Siegel, R. (Eds.). (1983). *Women Changing Therapy.* New York: Haworth Press.

Tanney, M.F., and Birk, J.M. (1976). "Women counselors for women clients? A review of the research." *The Counseling Psychologist, 6,* 28–32.

Walker, L.E. (Ed.) (1984). *Women and Mental Health Policy.* Beverly Hills, CA: Sage Publications.

Organizations Concerned With Women's Adjustment and Psychotherapy

Organization	*Address*
American Psychological Association	1200 17 Street, N.W. Washington, DC 20036
Association for Women in Psychology	Feminist Therapy c/o Ellyn Kashack Department of Psychology San Jose State University San Jose, CA 95192
Project on the Status and Education of Women	1818 R Street, N.W. Washington, DC 20009
Eating Disorders Clinic	Suite 200 315 West 57 New York, New York
South Oaks Hospital Alcoholism and Compulsive Gambling Programs	800-732-9809
Arms Acres Alcoholic Women's Program	800-227-2767 Outside New York: 800-431-1268
American Anorexia and Bulimia Association	133 Cedar Lane Teaneck, N.J. 07666
Anorexia and Bulimia Resource Center	2699 South Bayshore Suite 800E Florida 33133
Johns Hopkins Medical Institutions Eating and Weight Disorders Clinic	Meyer Building Suite 3-181 600 North Wolfe Street Baltimore, MD 21205
UCLA Neuropsychiatric Institute; Eating Disorders Program	760 Westwood Plaza Los Angeles, CA 90024
University of Cincinnati Medical Center Eating Disorders Clinic	Department of Psychiatry University of Cincinnati Cincinnati, OH 45267
Alcoholics Anonymous	National Headquarters Box 459 Grand Central Station New York, New York 10163
Woman to Woman	825 Third Avenue New York, New York 10022

Women for Sobriety

Box 618
Quakertown, PA 18951

Women in Crisis

133 West 21 Street
New York, New York 10011

Women's Alcoholism Center

3380 26 Street
San Francisco, CA 94110

Alcoholism Center for Women

1147 South Alvarado Street
Los Angeles, CA 90006

Asian Women's Health Project Center

Asian American Studies UCLA
Los Angeles, CA 90024

International Women's Health Coalition

1611 Connecticut Avenue, N.W.
Washington, DC 20009

Women's Occupational Health Resource
Center

Columbia University
School of Public Health
60 Haven Ave., B-1
New York, NY 10032

Audio-Visual material

Title	*Distributor*	*Description*
Rich, Thin, and Beautiful (Film)	Films, Inc. 1213 Wilmette Ave. Wilmette, IL 60091	Discusses society's demand that women fit into a male-defined concept of beauty and femininity.
Assertiveness Training for Women (Films)	American Personnel and Guidance 1607 New Hampshire Washington, DC 20009	High school and college women dealing with situations such as refusing dates, job interviews, canvassing for charity.
Bulimia (Film)	CRM/McGraw-Hill P.O. Box 641 Del Mar, CA 92014	Description of bulimia; an interview with Jane Fonda
Calling the Shots (Film)	Cambridge Documentary Films P.O. Box 385 Cambridge, MA 02139	Advertising of alcohol and its appeal to alcoholics.
The Last to Know (Film)	New Day Films 22 Riverview Dr. Wayne, NJ 07470	Description of women who are alcoholics.
Suzanne, Suzanne (Film)	Third World Newsreel 335 E 38th St. New York, NY 10018	Drug abuse and violence in Black families.

153

Popular Books

Title	Author/Editor	Publisher
Outrageous Acts and Everyday Rebellions	G. Steinem	Holt, Rinehart, & Winston
Fat is a Feminist Issue	S. Orbach	Berkeley
Passages	G. Sheehy	Bantam
Femininity	S. Brownmiller	Simon & Schuster
Codependence	A. Schaef	Winston
Women and Analysis	J. Strouse	Hall
Therapy with Women: A Feminist Philosophy of Treatment	S. Sturdivant	Spriner
The Obsession: Reflections on the Tyranny of Slenderness	K. Chernin	Colophone
New Our Bodies, Ourselves	Boston Women's Health Book Collective	Simon & Schuster
Mental Health and People of Color	J. Chunn, B. Dunston, and F. Ross-Sheriff	Howard
The Lavender Couch: A Consumer's Guide to Psychotherapy for Lesbians and Gay Men	M. Hall	Alyson

Guest Speakers for Presentations on Adjustment and Psychotherapy

    University Counseling Program

    Women's Center

    Alcoholics Anonymous

    Eating Disorders Clinic

    Psychology Department

    Counseling Department

    Therapist/Counselor

    Health Department

    Child and Family Therapist

    Drug Rehabilitation Center

Sample Discussion Questions

- Discuss the politics of deinstitutionalization for women clients.

- Discuss the similarities and differences between feminist and nonsexist therapy.

- Describe in detail the Broverman, *et al.* study of mental health practitioners. Critique this study, citing potential sources of bias in the research process.

- Discuss the limitations of androgyny as the exemplar of mental health for women.

- Discuss the DSM III-R. Describe the work of Caplan and Walker in creating the changes in this revision.

- Cite cultural similarities and differences in adjustment issues such as eating disorders.

- Discuss some perspectives on psychotherapy with elder women.

- Describe the issues involved in feminist therapy with lesbian women.

- Discuss the gender differences in the nature of body image.

- Discuss the interrelationships among gender-role expectations, power, and psychological distress.

Assumptions of Feminist Therapy*

The inferior status of women is due to their having less political and economic power than men. Power analysis is central to feminist thought and to feminist therapy.

The primary source of women's pathology is social, not personal.

The focus on environmental stress as a major source of pathology is not used as an avenue of escape from individual responsibility.

Feminist therapy is opposed to personal adjustment to social conditions; the goal is social and political change.

The therapist-client relationship is viewed as egalitarian.

Clients are encouraged to express anger and deal with it.

Women must be economically and psychologically autonomous.

Major differences between "appropriate" gender-role behaviors must disappear.

Relationships of lover, marriage, and friendship should be equal in personal power.

---

* See Gilbert, 1980 and Rawlings and Carter, 1977

Exercises

Exercise: Double Bind Issues in Women's Mental Health

Steps for Completing the Exercise:

1. Prepare three versions of a questionnaire for students to complete. One version is as follows:

   Describe what you believe a mentally healthy woman is like.

   Use the following characteristics in your description.

   1 = very true; 5 = very untrue.

   emotional

   gentle

   self-confident

   adventurous

   rough

   expressive of feelings

   active

   tactful

   passive

   not expressive of feelings

   blunt

   not adventurous

   unemotional

   not at all confident

2. Prepare the same description except substitute "man" and "adult" in these versions.

3. Ask one-third of the students to complete one form of the questionnaire.

4. Summarize the results for the class; notice whether the "adult" characteristics are closer to the "man" or "woman" descriptions.

5. Determine whether there is a difference based on students' sex.

6. Discuss therapists' bias against women and the double standard of mental health.

Sources:

Broverman, I.K., Broverman, D.M., Clarkson, F.E., Rosenkrantz, P.S., and Vogel, S.R. (1970). "Sex-role stereotypes and clinical judgments of mental health." *Journal of Consulting and Clinical Psychology, 34,* 1–7.

Smith, M.L. (1980). "Sex bias in counseling and psychotherapy." *Psychological Bulletin, 87,* 392–407.

Exercise: Community Mental Health Facilities

Steps for Completing the Exercise:

1. Divide the class into small groups of 4–5.

2. Have each group select a community mental health center.

3. Ask each group to interview a person at the center about the services they offer for women.

4. Ask each group to prepare a brief annotated description of the center.

5. Distribute copies of the lists to the entire class.

6. Discuss benefits of these centers to women.

Exercise: Media Portrayal of Ideal Physical Femininity

Steps for Completing the Exercise:

1. Ask students to read the advertisements addressed to women in the back of magazines such as *Cosmopolitan, Vogue, Bazaar.*

2. Have students bring to class the advertisements for weight loss, bust enlargement, hair beautifiers, elegant lingerie, make-up, soft skin.

3. Ask students to describe the direct and indirect messages portrayed in these advertisements.

4. Discuss how the emphasis on thinness has replaced corsets and footbinding in the attempt to have women fit into a male-defined definition of beauty and femininity.

5. Ask students to list women in popular television shows who are even a few pounds overweight.

6. Have the students list men in television shows who are overweight.

7. Discuss whether there are age, racial, and ethnic differences in the advertisements and television programs.

8. Discuss the implications of a different portrayal of women in the media on women's eating disorders.

Sources:

Orbach, S. (1978). *Fat is a Feminist Issue.* New York: Berkeley.

Wooley, S.C., and Wooley, O.W. (1979). "Obesity and women: II. A neglected feminist topic." *Women's Studies International Quarterly, 2,* 81–92.

Part 5

Achievement and Work

Chapter 7

Achievement and Achievement Motivation

Sample Outline

Theoretical Issues

> Motive to approach success
>
> Motive to avoid failure
>
> Expectancy value
>
> Motive to avoid success
>
> Causal attributions of success and failure
>
> Mentoring and being mentored
>
> Direct achieving style and relational achieving style

Methodological Issues

> Thematic apperception test and scoring of need achievement
>
> Projective hypothesis
>
> Fantasy based cue *vs.* motive strength
>
> Objective measures of the motive to avoid success
>
> Idiographic measure of success and fear of success
>
> Psychometric properties of measuring instruments

Developmental and Cultural Issues

> Continuities and discontinuities in the socialization of achievement motivation
>
> Career/vocational development
>
> School achievement
>
> Dropouts and underachievers

Attitudes toward school

Gifted children and adolescents

Queen Bees

Women in male-dominated college majors and occupations

Parental and teacher influences on achievement and career development

Re-entry students

Conceptual Issues

Femininity/achievement incompatibility

Masculine bias of measuring instruments

Masculine bias of definition of achievement

Constructivist interpretation of the motive to avoid success

Achievement expressed through affiliation

Counseling gifted and talented women

Penalties for women's success

Competition *vs.* cooperation

Affirmative Action

Sexual and gender harassment

Sample References

Theoretical/Conceptual Issues

Almquist, E.M., and Angrist, S. (1970). "Career salience and atypicality of occupational choice among college women." *Journal of Marriage and the Family, 32*, 242–249.

Astin, H.S., Suniewick, N., and Dweck, S. (1974). *Women: A Bibliography on Their Education and Careers.* NY: Behavioral Publishers.

Betz, N., and Fitzgerald, L. (1987). *The Career Psychology of Women.* New York: Academic Press.

Canavan-Gumpert, D., Garner, K., and Gumpert, P. (1978). *The Success-Fearing Personality: Theory and Research with Implications for the Social Psychology of Achievement.* Lexington, MA: D. C. Heath & Company.

Covington, M.V., and Berry, R.G. (1976). *Self-Worth and School Learning.* NY: Holt, Rinehart, & Winston.

Deaux, K., and Emswiller, T. (1974). "Explanations of successful performance on sex-linked tasks: What is skill for the male is luck for the female." *Journal of Personality and Social Psychology, 29,* 80–85.

Douvan, E. (1976). "The role of models in women's professional development." *Psychology of Women Quarterly, 1,* 5–20.

Eccles, J. (1983). "Expectancies, values, and academic behaviors." In J.T. Spence (Ed.), *Achievement and Achievement Motives.* San Francisco: W. H. Freeman.

Feldman, S.D. (1974). *Escape from the Doll's House: Women in Graduate and Professional School Education.* NY: McGraw-Hill.

Fitzgerald, L.F., and Betz, N.E. (1983). "Issues in the vocational psychology of women." In W.B. Walsh and S.H. Osipow (Eds.) *Handbook of Vocational Psychology.* Vol. 1. Hillsdale, NJ: Lawrence Erlbaum Associates, Publishers, pp. 83–159.

Fitzgerald, L.F., and Crites, J.O. (1980). "Toward a career psychology of women: What do we know? What do we need to know?" *Journal of Counseling Psychology, 27,* 44–62.

Frieze, I.H., Fisher, J., McHugh, M.C., and Valle, V.A. (1978). "Attributing the causes of success and failure: Internal and external barriers to achievement in women." In J. Sherman and F. Denmark (Eds.), *Psychology of Women: Future Directions of Research.* NY: Psychological Dimensions.

Gilligan, C. (1982). *In a Different Voice.* Cambridge: Harvard University Press.

Horner, M.S. (1968). "Sex differences in achievement motivation and performance in competitive and noncompetitive situations." (Doctoral dissertation, University of Michigan). *Dissertation Abstracts International, 30,* 407B.

Jackaway, R., and Teevan, R. (1976). "Fear of failure and fear of success: Two dimensions of the same motive." *Sex Roles, 2,* 283–293.

Kaufman, D.R., and Richardson, B.L. (1982). *Achievement and Women: Challenging the Assumptions.* NY: The Free Press.

Lenney, E. (1977). "Women's self-confidence in achievement setting." *Psychological Bulletin, 84,* 1–13.

Lipman-Blumen, J., Handley-Isaksen, A., and Leavitt, H.J. (1983). "Achieving styles in men and women: A model, an instrument, and some findings." In J.T. Spence (Ed.), *Achievement and Achievement Motives.* San Francisco: W. H. Freeman, pp. 151–204.

McClelland, D.C., Atkinson, J.W., Clark, R.A., and Lowell, E.L. (1953). *The Achievement Motive.* NY: Appelton-Century-Crofts.

Mednick, M., Tangri, S., and Hoffman, L.W. (Eds.). (1975). *Women and Achievement: Social and Motivational Analyses.* NY: Wiley.

Merriam, S. (1983). "Mentors and proteges: A critical review of the literature." *Adult Education Quarterly, 33,* 161–173.

Osipow, S.H. (Ed.) (1975). *Emerging Women: Career Analysis and Outlooks.* Columbus, Ohio: Merrill.

Rich, S.L., and Phillips, A. (Eds.). (1985). *Women's Experience and Education.* Cambridge, MA: Harvard Educational Review.

Sassen, G. (1980). "Success anxiety in women: A constructivist interpretation of its source and significance." *Harvard Educational Review, 50,* 13–24.

Shamanoff, G.A. (1985). "The women mentor project: A sharing approach." *Roeper Review, 7,* 163–164.

Spence, J.T. (Ed.) (1983). *Achievement and Achievement Motives.* San Francisco, CA: W.H. Freeman.

Stein, A.H., and Bailey, M.M. (1973). "The socialization of achievement orientation in females." *Psychological Bulletin, 80,* 345–366.

Walsh, W.B., and Osipow, S.H. (Eds.). (1983). *Handbook of Vocational Psychology.* Vol. 1. Hillsdale, NJ: Lawrence Erlbaum Associates, Publishers.

Wirtenberg, T., & Nakamura, C. (1976). "Education: Barrier or boon to changing occupational roles of women?" *Journal of Social Issues, 32,* 225–231.

Methodological Issues

Fogel, R., and Paludi, M.A. (1984). "Fear of success and failure or norms for achievement?" *Sex Roles, 10,* 431–434.

Gravenkemper, S.A., and Paludi, M.A. (1983). "Fear of success revisited: Introducing an ambiguous cue." *Sex Roles, 9,* 897–900.

McClelland, D.C. (1958). "Methods of measuring human motivation." In J.W. Atkinson (Ed.), *Motives in Fantasy, Action, and Society: A Method of Assessment and Study.* Princeton, N.J.: Van Nostrand.

Monahan, L., Kuhn, D., and Shaver, P. (1974). "Intrapsychic *vs.* cultural explanations of the fear of success motive." *Journal of Personality and Social Psychology, 29,* 60–64.

Paludi, M.A. (1984). "Psychometric properties and underlying assumptions of four objective measures of fear of success." *Sex Roles, 10,* 765–781.

Paludi, M.A., and Fankell-Hauser, J. (1986). "An idiographic approach to the study of women's achievement striving." *Psychology of Women Quarterly, 10,* 89–100.

Zuckerman, M., and Allison, S.N. (1976). "An objective measure of fear of success: Construction and validation." *Journal of Personality Assessment, 40,* 422–430.

Zuckerman, M., and Wheeler, L. (1975). "To dispel fantasies about the fantasy-based measure of fear of success." *Psychological Bulletin, 82,* 932–946.

Developmental and Cultural Issues

Dolny, C. (1985). "University of Toronto schools' gifted students' career and family plans." *Roeper Review, 7,* 160–162.

Fleming, J. (1978). "Fear of success, achievement-related motives and the behavior in black college women." *Journal of Personality, 46,* 694–716.

Garbarino, J., and Asp, C.E. (1981). *Successful Schools and Competent Students.* Lexington, MA: Heath.

Kelly, G.P., & Elliott, C.M. (Eds.). (1982). *Women's Education in the Third World: Comparative Perspectives.* Albany, NY: State University of New York Press.

Lavach, J.F., and Lanier, H.B. (1975). "The motive to avoid success in 7th, 8th, 9th, and 10th grade high achieving girls." *Journal of Educational Research, 68,* 216–218.

Puryear, G.R., and Mednick, M.S. (1974). "Black militancy, affective attachment, and the fear of success in black college women." *Journal of Consulting and Clinical Psychology, 42,* 263–266.

Rich, S.L., & Phillips, A. (Eds.). (1985). *Women's Experience and Education.* Cambridge, MA: Harvard Educational Review.

Weishaar, M.E., Green, B.J., and Craighead, L.W. (1981). "Primary influences of initial vocational choices for college women." *Journal of Vocational Behavior, 18,* 67–78.

Pamphlets, Reports, and Magazines

Gender-balanced curriculum
    Oswald Mayers
    Project Director
    Department of English
    College of St. Benedict
    St. Joseph, MN 56374

Ideas for gender balancing the college curriculum
    Janet Polansky
    Chair, Women's Studies Program
    126 D
    Harvey Hall
    University of Wisconsin-Stout
    Menomonie, WI 54751

On teaching and learning-professor's sex: Impact on classroom discussions
    C.G. Krupnick
    Harvard-Danforth Center for Teaching and Learning
    11 University Hall
    Harvard University
    Cambridge, MA 02138

Readings about women's concerns
    Susan Williamson
    Swarthmore College Library
    Swarthmore, PA 19081

Cross-cultural perspectives and women's experiences
    Frances Maher
    Professor of Education
    Wheaton College
    Norton, MA 02766

The classroom climate: A chilly one for women?
    Project on the Status and Education of Women
    Association of American Colleges
    1818 R St. NW
    Washington, DC 20009

Black re-entry females: Their concerns and needs
    Mildred Dalton Henry
    National Association of Women Deans, Administrators, and Counselors
    1325 18 St. NW
    Washington, DC 20036

Beyond equals: To encourage the participation of women in mathematics
    The Math/Science Resource Center
    Mills College
    Oakland, CA 94613

Magazines:

Success: The magazine for achievers

Savvy

Working Women

Working Mothers

Roeper Review: A Journal on Gifted Education: February-March, 1980, vol. 2. Special Issue: *The Gifted Female*

Contents:

M. Blaubergs: Sex-role stereotyping and gifted girls

C. Callahan: The gifted girl: An anomaly?

J. Navarre: Is what is good for the gander, good for the goose? Should gifted girls receive differential treatment?

E. Hall: Sex differences in IQ development for gifted students

C. Mills: Sex role-related personality correlates of intellectual abilities in adolescents

R. Kirschenbaum: Combating sexism in the preschool environment

Organizations Concerned with Women's Achievement

Organization	Address
National Women's Studies Association	University of Maryland 203 Behavioral and Social Sciences Building College Park, MD 20742
Association for Black Women in Higher Education	30 Limerick Dr. Albany, NY 12204
National Organization for Women	425 13 St. N.W. Suite 723 Washington, DC 20004
Project on the Status and Education of Women	1818 R Street, NW Washington, DC 20009
National Network of Minority Women in Science	Association for the Advancement of Science 1776 Massachusetts Avenue, NW Washington, DC 20036
Education Development Center	55 Chapel Street Newton, MA 02160
Adult Educational Association of the USA	810 18 St. NW Washington, DC 20006

American Association of Community and Junior Colleges	Center for Women's Opportunities One Dupont Circle Washington, DC 20036
Hispanic American Career Educational Resources, Inc.	115 West 30 St. Room 900 New York, NY 10001
American Council on Education	Office of Women in Higher Education 1 Dupont Circle Suite 829 Washington, DC 20036
National Institute of Education	Minorities and Women's Programs 1200 19 St. NW Washington, DC 20208
National University Continuing Education Association	Division of Women's Education One Dupont Circle Suite 360 Washington, DC 20036
Center for the Study, Education, and Advancement of Women	University of California Building T-9, Room 112 Berkeley, CA 94720
American Educational Research Association	Special Interest Group on Research on Women and Education 1230 17 St., NW Washington, DC 20036

Financial Assistance for Women

In addition to information that may be obtained from college and university financial aid offices, the following information may be useful:

American Geophysical Union
2000 Florida Ave., NW
Washington, DC 20009

The Business and Professional Women's Foundation
2012 Massachusetts Ave., NW
Washington, DC 20036

Soroptimist International of the Americas
1616 Walnut Street
Philadelphia, PA 19190

National Women's Studies Association
University of Maryland
College Park, MD 20742

National Association of Black Women Attorneys
3711 Macomb St. NW
Washington, DC 20016

American Home Economics Association Foundation
2010 Massachusetts Ave., NW
Washington, DC 20036

Audio-Visual Material

Title	Distributor	Description
Women in Sports (Film)	Pyramid Box 496 Media, PA 19063	Reviews women's participation in sports and opinions of women athletes. A discussion of Title IX is also presented.
Deal Me in—Women in Male-Dominated Jobs (Film)	Florida Department of Community Affairs	Reviews women's achievement and career decision making.
An Acquired Taste (Film)	Filmakers Library 124 E. 40th St. New York, NY 10016	Examines Americans' fixation with being number 1.
Lives of Eminent Women (Films)	Extension Media Center University of California Distribution Desk Berkeley, CA 94720	The lives of the following women are documented: Margaret Sanger, Virginia Woolf, Harriet Tubman, Gertrude Stein.
What's a Nice Girl Like You Doing in a Place Like This? (Slide Presentation)	Anne Thorton 1611 Baker San Francisco, CA 92117	Interviews with students at Stanford University about the reactions of faculty and students to their being enrolled in a graduate business school.
Back to School, Back to Work (Film)	American Personnel and Guidance Association Film Department 1607 New Hampshire Ave. N.W. Washington, DC 20009	Vignettes about women's decision to undertake two roles.
Discrimination Against Women in Educational Textbooks (Slide Presentation)	Education Committee San Fernando Volley NOW P.O. Box 20 Canoga Park, CA 91303	A description of stereotypic and sexist portrayal of women in texts.
Great Women Artists, Past and Present (Slide Presentation)	Women's Studies Program California State College Sonoma Rohnert Park, CA 94928	Vignettes about the artistic contributions made by women.
Great Women of America (Film)	Classroom World 22 Glenwood Ave. Raleigh, NC 27603	Portrayals of the following women: Helen Keller, Mary Wells, Susan B. Anthony, Clara Barton, Claire Booth Luce, Louisa May Alcott.

Popular Books

Title	Author/Editor	Publisher
Death in a Tenured Position	A. Cross	Ballantine
Death of a Salesman	A. Miller	Viking Press
Powerplay	M. Cunningham	Linden Press
Women on Top	J. Adams	Hawthorn
Three Women: Lives of Sex and Genius	W. Sorrell	Bobbs-Merrill
Working it Out: 23 women writers, artists, scientists and scholars talk about their lives and work	S. Ruddick and P. Daniels	Pantheon
Angela Davis: An Autobiography	A. Davis	Random House
Uncommon Women	J. Kufrin	New Century
Women of Crisis: Lives of Struggle and Hope	R. Coles and J. Coles	Delacorte
Art Talk: Conversations with 12 Women Artists	C. Nemser	Scribner
The Women of Psychology	G. Stevens and G. Gardner	Schenkman
A Voice in her Tribe	I. Stewart	Ballena

Guest Speakers for Presentations on Achievement and Achievement Motivation

Career Planning and Placement Center
Department of Special Education: Gifted Children and Adolescents
Continuing Education
Affirmative Action Office
Curriculum Development
Administrative and Professional Women's Organization
College Honors Association
Members of the School Board
Elementary and Secondary School Teachers
Special Olympics Representative
Housecare Workers

Sample Discussion Questions

- Describe the causal attributions women make about their successes and failures. Note any developmental discontinuities in this process.

- To date, psychologists' definitions of achievement have been limited. In what ways? Discuss your answer citing relevant research.

- What are some of the opportunities and obstacles in education for women? Be sure to deal with re-entry women's concerns.

- Trace the history of education in your family. How do these experiences compare to your own. Cite reasons for any discrepancies.

- Discuss sociopsychological and structural factors affecting women's achievement and career pathways.

- Cite some of the research on women of Color that challenges some previously accepted findings on women's causal attributions for success and failure as well as fear of success.

- What are the criteria for labeling an individual as "gifted?" Do you see any potential sexism in this process?

- Discuss the difference between a role model and a mentor. Have you had a role model? A mentor?

- Discuss the difference between the direct achieving style and the relational achieving style. Which one do you believe better describes your achieving style? Why?

- Why has most of the research on women's achievement been concerned with women in male-populated jobs? Describe the bias against female-populated occupations.

Exercises

Exercise: Goals of a College Education

Steps for Completing the Exercise:

1. Divide the class into small groups of four people.

2. Each member of the group should generate as many ideas or associations as possible on the topic of college education. Ask students to think about what education means to them. Have them think about what a college education should include or avoid, how it affects their personal life, and any other ideas they may have about education.

3. List all the ideas that are generated.

4. After each group has exhausted its ideas, each group member should review the recorded list, eliminate whatever they do not want included in their own personal list and write down all the remaining ideas.

5. When they finish, review the list to see if it includes everything they do want and does not include anything they don't want.

6. When all members of the group have finished, ask students to share the lists that each have written. Discuss why they included certain ideas in their personal list and eliminated others. Did they combine ideas in a way that the others didn't? Discuss why. Did they make different interpretations of what the ideas meant? Did they consider the ideas in a different way than other members of their group? Did they want to make any changes in their list after listening to other members of their group? Why or why not?

Exercise: Re-entry Career Issues

Steps for Completing the Exercise:

1. Discuss re-entry status and the mid-life woman as student.
   Reference: Schlossberg, N. (1984). "The mid-life woman as student." In G. Baruch and J. Brooks-Gunn (Eds.) *Women in Midlife.* (pp. 315–339). New York: Plenum.

2. Ask students to arrange an interview with a professional in their field of study who was a re-entry student.

173

3. Have students ask these individuals about the following issues:
   a. age at which they entered college
   b. difficulties they encountered from family members, teachers' expectations, etc.
   c. stresses associated with their work
   d. role models and/or mentors who helped advance their career
   e. the blocks in themselves and in the world they had to overcome in order to achieve their goals

4. Ask students to discuss their interview responses with the class.

5. Look for similarities and differences in interview responses due to sex, race, age, SES, ethnicity, religious background, and occupation.

6. Discuss practical implications of modifying the college curriculum for re-entry students.

Exercise: Role Models and Mentors

Steps for Completing the Exercise:

1. Administer the items from the role model/mentor survey developed by Paludi, 1985. (See Table.)

2. Ask students to write 1–2 major issues that the material raised in their minds.

3. Post these issues.

4. Establish discussion topic priorities.

5. Allocate the remaining time to the topic of one or two issues.

6. Ask the students to form a fishbowl(s) with an outer and an inner group.

7. Have the inner group discuss the issue for 8–12 minutes. Assign a recorder to take notes from the discussion.

8. Allow 6–8 minutes at the end for those students in the outer group to make comments.

9. Switch the composition of the inner and outer group for each issue.

10. Post the major conclusions that are drawn from each discussion.

11. Lecture about the impact of role models and mentors on career development. Points to consider:
    a. masculine bias in definition of mentor
    b. distinction between mentor and role model
    c. drawbacks to having a mentor
    d. cross-sex mentoring
    e. establishing mentoring programs

Table

Items from Paludi Role Model/Mentor Survey:

1. During elementary, junior high, and high school, who was the person or persons you wanted to be like? That is, who did you try to model yourself after? Was this person male or female?

2. At the present time whom do you consider a role model? Is this person male or female?

3. Do you believe you can achieve advancement in your career by the help of this person? Explain your answer.

4. Do you consider whether an individual is male or female an important characteristic of someone you would like to model yourself after? Explain your answer.

5. Which of the following career competencies do you believe are important for a mentor? Indicate your opinions by placing check mark in the space(s) you believe are appropriate.

Communication Skills

verbal skills (expressing self well)   _____

public speaking skills (thinks easy on their feet)   _____

writing skills (writes concisely)   _____

Interpersonal Skills

handling negative responses from others (doesn't get defensive)   _____

expresses anger (practices before responding)   _____

relates to colleagues (tact, diplomacy)   _____

handles sexist behavior and attitudes   _____

175

finds support (works to support others; establishes support groups) _____

Political Skills

knowledge of the system _____

anticipates consequences of actions _____

promotes oneself (develops strategies to get work known) _____

visibility behaviors (conference attendance; present papers) _____

promotes women _____

Organizational Skills

chairs committees _____

takes initiative in groups _____

administrative skills _____

Job Specific Skills

knowledge of subject matter _____

teaching skills (concerned about students; excited about topics) _____

research skills _____

publication skills _____

funding, grant writing skills _____

research creativity _____

Adaptive Cognitive Strategies

positive self-talk (doesn't accept responsibility for problems that are not their fault) _____

copes with rejection _____

realistic self-appraisal _____

self-acceptance _____

copes with gender-role expectations _____

inhibits negative self-talk _____

Adapted from Hackett, G., Betz, N.E., and Doty, M.S. (1985). "The development of a taxonomy of career competencies for professional women." *Sex Roles, 12,* 393–409.

6. How do *you* define a role model?

7. How do *you* define a mentor?

Exercise: Biographical Interviewing of Achievement Striving

Steps for Completing the Exercise

1. Ask students to answer for themselves the interview items presented below.

2. Ask students to establish discussion topic priorities.

3. Post responses to the top two questions from the interview items.

4. Ask the class to form a fishbowl(s) with an outer group and an inner group.

5. Leave one or two empty chairs in the inner circle. Those students in the outer circle who have something to say can be allowed to enter the inner circle and take part. They leave the inner circle when they believe they have exhausted their input.

6. Allow the inner group to discuss the responses to the interview items for 10–15 minutes.

7. Allow 10 minutes at the end for those in the outer group to make comments.

8. Post the major conclusions that are drawn from the discussions.

9. Compare the contrast the students' responses with the data obtained by Paludi and Fankell-Hauser (1986). Discuss rival hypotheses for the similarities and differences in results obtained.

Biographical Interview Items

1. What, specifically, do you want to accomplish in the next few years?

2. What specific steps do you plan to take to achieve these goals?

3. What blocks in yourself will you have to overcome to achieve these goals?

4. What blocks in the world will you have to overcome to achieve these goals?

5. How do you feel about the possibility of achieving these goals? Of failing to achieve them?

6. How do your parents feel about the possibility of you achieving these goals? About you failing to achieve them?

7. How does your spouse (mate) feel about your achieving these goals?

8. How do your children feel about you achieving these goals?

9. How do your men acquaintances feel about you achieving these goals?

10. How do your women acquaintances feel about you achieving these goals?

11. Who, if anyone, are the people (or person) you would like to be like? That is, who are the people you try to model yourself after? Describe the different role models you've had over the course of your life.

12. Have you ever been in a situation where you were about to succeed at something and wondered if it was worth it or got afraid of your success or something it might produce?
Source: Paludi, M.A., and Fankell-Hauser, J. (1986). "An idiographic approach to the study of women's achievement striving." *Psychology of Women Quarterly, 10,* 89–100.

Exercise: Understanding Academic Choice

Steps for Completing the Exercise:

1. Discuss girls' cultural milieu, goals, aptitudes, grades, expectancies, and attributions. Use Jacquelynne Eccles' model of academic choice while describing these expectancies and values.
   Sample Reference: Meece, J., and Eccles-Parsons, J. (1982). "Sex differences in math achievement: Toward a model of academic choice." *Psychological Bulletin, 91,* 324–348.
   Points to Highlight:
   a. gender differences in math ability do not appear consistently until the tenth grade;
   b. concurrently, girls do not enroll in high school math courses as frequently as do boys;
   c. after college, women do not have as many mathematical skills as men because they have not been taking math;

    d. mathematical skills are important to career success;

    e. major questions to address is not whether women have less ability in mathematics but rather why do women avoid taking courses in mathematics;

    f. how can we help women to take more math courses so as to help them expand their career choice?

2. Have the students trace through the model for themselves. This can be done in class or as a homework exercise for the next class meeting.

3. Ask the students whether Eccles' model predicts why they did or did not continue taking math courses in college. Ask the students to tell you 1–2 central issues that the material raised in their minds.

4. Post the issues generated in step 3.

5. Ask the students to self-select into the issues they prefer to discuss.

6. Select a recorder for each group.

7. Allow 15–20 minutes for the groups to discuss the issues. Have the recorder jot down the content of the discussion. If any student tires of the discussion in one group, he/she should be encouraged to rotate to other discussion groups.

8. Allow 10 minutes for each group to indicate what they discussed and 2 major conclusions that were drawn.

9. Post conclusions from each group.

10. Have the students look for some individual differences and similarities, *e.g.*, ethnicity, race, age, sex, gender-role orientation, SES, family lifestyle (*i.e.*, divorced, widowed, single-parent).

11. Inquire about any enrichment experiences the students may have had from their parent(s) and teachers.

12. Discuss the practical implications of Eccles' model.

Chapter 8

Women and Work

Sample Outline

Women's career choices

    attitudes

    preferences

Factors affecting women's decision to work

    age

    education

    ethnicity

    family variables

    mobility

Division of labor by sex

    skilled labor

    self-employment

    volunteering

    domestic wage laborer

    factory worker

    pink collar worker

    professional

Evaluations of women's performance

    pro-male bias

    gender-role congruence

    level of qualification of performance

Developmental issues in careers and work

    timing of work

    mid-career changes

    multiple careers over the life-span

    re-entry women

    retirement

Ethnic minority women and work

    femininity-achievement compatibility

    sex-differential schooling

    career paths

Social support for women's careers

    mentoring and being mentored

    unions

    networks

    professional organizations

    families

    friends

    government and law

    protective legislation

Organizational rewards for women

    salary

    promotions

    social networks

    comfort

    intrinsic rewards

Discrimination against women in the workplace

    prejudicial attitudes

    discriminatory behavior

sexual and gender harassment

attributional biases

self-serving biases

Integrating work and family life

single mothers

dual wage couples

effects of maternal employment on the family context

child care

on-site day care

single women

voluntary childlessness

Toward a synthesis of women, careers, and work

economic necessity

rising educational attainments

changing demographic trends

changing employment trends

approaches to change

moral commitment and life choices

renegotiating the definition and boundaries of achievement

Sample References

General

Betz, N., and Fitzgerald, L. (1987). *The Career Psychology of Women.* New York: Academic Press.

Fox, M.F., and Hesse-Biber, S. (1984). *Women at Work.* Palo Alto, Calif.: Mayfield.

Kahn-Hut, R., Daniels, K., and Colvard, R. (1982). *Women and Work.* New York: Oxford University Press.

Larwood, L., and Gutek, B.A. (1984). "Women at work in the USA." In M.J. Davidson and C.L. Cooper (Eds.), *Women at Work* (pp. 237–267). Chchester, England: Wiley.

Nivea, V.F., & Gutek, B.A. (1981). *Women and Work: A Psychological Perspective.* New York: Praeger.

Women's Career Choices

Angrist, S.S., and Almquist, E.M. (1975). *Careers and Contingencies: How College Women Juggle with Gender.* New York: Dunellen.

Betz, N.E., and Hackett, G. (1981). "The relationship of career-related self-efficacy expectations to perceived career options in college women and men." *Journal of Counseling Psychology, 28,* 399–410.

Betz, N.E., and Fitzgerald, L.F. (1987). *The Career Psychology of Women.* New York: Academic Press.

Cartwright, L.K. (1977). "Continuity and non-continuity in the careers of a sample of young women physicians." *Journal of the American Medical Women's Association, 32,* 316–321.

Diamond, E.E. (1984, August). "Theories of career development and the reality of women at work." Paper presented at the meeting of the American Psychological Association, Toronto, CN.

Fitzgerald, L.F. (1986). "On the essential relations between education and work." *Journal of Vocational Behavior, 28,* 254–284.

Fitzgerald, L.F., and Betz, N.E. (1983). "Issues in the vocational psychology of women." In W.B. Walsh and S.H. Osipow (Eds.), *Handbook of Vocational Psychology (vol. 1).* Hillsdale, N.J.: Erlbaum.

Fitzgerald, L.F., and Cherpas, C.C. (1985). "On the reciprocal relationship between gender and occupation: Rethinking the assumptions concerning masculine career development." *Journal of Vocational Behavior, 27,* 109–122.

Gutek, B. (Ed.) (1979). *New directions for Education, Work, and Careers: Enhancing Women's Career Development.* San Francisco: Jossey-Bass.

Laws, J.L. (1976). "Work aspiration of women: False leads and new starts." *Signs, 1,* 33–50.

Perun, P. J., and Bielby, D.D. (1981). "Towards a model of female occupational behavior: A human development approach." *Psychology of Women Quarterly,6,* 234–252.

Division of Labor by Sex

Bourne, P.G., and Wikler, N.J. (1982). "Commitment and the cultural mandate: Women in medicine." In R. Kahn-Hut, A.K. Daniel, and R. Colvard (Eds.), *Women and Work: Problems and Perspectives.* New York: Oxford University Press.

Deaux, K., and Ullman, J.C. (1983). *Women of Steel.* New York: Praeger.

Kanter, R.M. (1977). *Men and Women of the Corporation.* New York: Basic Books.

Lees, S.H. (1986, March). "Technology and change in Israel farm women's productive roles." Paper presented at the Conference on Gender Issues in Farming Systems Research and Extension, Gainesville, Fl.

Roos, P.A. (1985). *Gender and Work: A Comparative Analysis of Industrial Societies.* Albany, NY: SUNY Press.

Warr, P., and Parry, G. (1982). "Paid employment and women's psychological well-being." *Psychological Bulletin, 91,* 498–516.

Evaluations of Women's Performance

Bronstein, P., Black, L., Pfennig, J., and White, A. (1986). "Getting academic jobs: Are women equally qualified—and equally successful?" *American Psychologist, 41,* 318–322.

Fidell, L.S. (1976). "Empirical verification of sex discrimination in hiring practices in psychology." In R. Unger and F. Denmark (Eds.), *Woman: Dependent or Independent Variable?* (pp. 779–782). New York: Psychological Dimensions.

Firth, M. (1982). "Sex Discrimination in job opportunities for women." *Sex Roles, 8,* 891–901.

Major, B., McFarlin, D.B., and Gagnon, D. (1984). "Overworked and underpaid: On the nature of gender differences in personal entitlement." *Journal of Personality and Social Psychology, 47,* 1399–1412.

Paludi, M.A., and Strayer, L.A. (1985). "What's in an author's name? Differential evaluations of performance as a function of author's name." *Sex Roles, 12,* 353–361.

Yogev, S. (1983). "Judging the professional woman: Changing research, changing values." *Psychology of Women Quarterly, 7,* 219–234.

Developmental Issues in Careers and Work

Fox, J.S. (1977). "Effects of retirement and former work life on women's adaptation in old age." *Journal of Gerontology, 32,* 196–202.

Ethnic Minority Women and Work

Almquist, E., and Wehrle-Rinhorn, J.L. (1978). "The doubly disadvantaged: Minority women in the labor force." In H. Stromberg and S. Harkness.

(Eds.), *Women Working: Theories and Facts in Perspective.* Palo Alto, Calif.: Mayfield.

Feree, M.M. (1985). "Between two worlds: German feminist approaches to working-class women and work." *Signs, 10,* 517–536.

Gronseth, E. (1978). "Work sharing: A Norwegian example." In R. Rapoport and R. Rapoport (Eds.), *Working Couples.* New York: Harper.

Joseph, G. (1983). *Women at Work: The British experience.* Atlantic Highlands, NJ: Humanities Press.

McHenry, P.C., Hamdorf, K.G., Walters, C.M., and Murray, C.I. (1985). "Family and job influences on role satisfaction of employed rural mothers." *Psychology of Women Quarterly, 9,* 242–257.

U.S. Department of Labor (1977). *Minority Women Workers: A Statistical Overview.* Washington: U.S. Government Printing Office.

Woody, B., and Malson, M. (1984). *In Crisis: Low Income Black Employed Women in the U.S. Workplace.* Working paper No. 131. Wellesley College Center for Research on Women.

Social Support for Women's Careers

Berch, B. (1982). *The Endless Day: The Political Economy of Women and Work.* New York: Harcourt Brace Jovanovich.

Beutler, M.E. (1980). *Networking, Sponsorship, and Peer Support: A Collection of Readings.* Austin: Southwest Educational Development Laboratory.

Douvan, E. (1976). "The role of models in women's professional development." *Psychology of Women Quarterly, 1,* 5–20.

Organizational Rewards for Women

Corcoran, M., Duncan, G.J., and Hill, M.S. (1984). "The economic fortunes of women and children: Lessons from the panel study of income dynamics." *Signs, 10,* 232–248.

Crosby, F. (1982). *Relative Deprivation and Working Women.* New York: Oxford University Press.

Englander-Golden, P., and Barton, G. (1983). "Sex differences in absence from work: A reinterpretation." *Psychology of Women Quarterly, 8,* 185–188.

Gold, M.E. (1983). *A Dialogue on Comparable Worth.* Ithaca, NY: ILR Press.

Hartmann, H.I., and Treiman, D.J. (Eds.) (1981). *Women, Work, and Wages.* Washington: National Academy Press.

Pines, A., and Kafry, P. (1981). "Tedium in the life and work of professional women as compared with men." *Sex Roles, 7,* 963–977.

Discrimination Against Women in the Workplace (also see Chapter on Victimization)

Gutek, B. (1985). *Sex and the Workplace.* San Francisco, Calif.: Jossey-Bass.

Gutek, B.A., and Morasch, B. (1982). "Sex-ratios, sex-role spillover, and sexual harassment of women at work." *Journal of Social Issues, 38,* 55–74.

Levine, M.P., & Leonard, R. (1984). "Discrimination against lesbians in the work force." *Signs, 9,* 700–710.

Little-Bishop, S., Seidler-Feller, D.L., and Opaluch, R.E. (1982). "Sexual harassment in the workplace as a function of initiator's status: The case of airline personnel." *Journal of Social Issues, 38,* 137–148.

Livingston, J.A. (1982). "Responses to sexual harassment on the job: Legal, organizational, and individual actions." *Journal of Social Issues, 38,* 5–22.

O'Leary, V.E. (1974). "Some attitudinal barriers to occupational aspirations in women." *Psychological Bulletin, 81,* 809–816.

Schneider, B.E. (1982). "Consciousness about sexual harassment among heterosexual and lesbian women workers." *Journal of Social Issues, 38,* 75–98.

Shullman, S.L., Bailey, N.J., Richards, M.M., Loucka, P.A., Nicholson, J.A., and Bernard, L. (1986, August). "Sexual harassment of women professionals: Empirical study of power issues." Paper presented at the Annual Meeting of the American Psychological Association, Washington, DC.

Yoder, J.D., and Crumption, P.L. (1986, August). "Gatekeepers of the jobmarket in psychology." Paper presented at the Meeting of the American Psychological Association, Washington, DC.

Toward a Synthesis of Women, Careers, and Work

Bianchi, S., and Spain, D. (1983). *American Women: Three Decades of Change.* Washington: U.S. Government Printing Office.

Ferber, M.A. (1982). "Women and work: Issues of the 1980s." *Signs, 8,* 273–295.

Laws, J.L. (1978). "Work motivation and work behavior of women: New perspectives." In J.A. Sherman and F.L. Denmark, (Eds.), *The Psychology of Women: Future Directions in Research* (pp. 287–342). New York: Psychological Dimensions.

Peterson, J.L. (1979). "Work and socioeconomic life-cycles: An Agenda for longitudinal research." *Monthly Labor Review, 102,* 23–27.

U.S. Department of Labor. (1983). *Time of Change: 1983 Handbook on Women Workers (Bulletin 298).* Washington, DC: U.S. Government Printing Office.

Vetter, L. (1978). "Career counseling for women." In L.S. Hansen and R.S. Rapoza (Eds.), *Career Development and Counseling of Women* (pp. 7–26). Springfield, IL: Charles C. Thomas.

Integrating Work and Family Life

Anderson-Kulman, R., and Paludi, M.A. (1986). "Working mothers and the family context: Predicting positive coping." *Journal of Vocational Behavior, 28,* 241–253.

Borman, K.M., Quarm, D., and Gideonse, S. (Eds.) (1984). *Women in the Workplace: Effects on Families.* Norwood, NJ: Ablex.

Cherlin, A. (1980). "Postponing marriage: The influence of young women's work expectations." *Journal of Marriage and the Family, 42,* 355–365.

Etaugh, C. (1980). "Effects of nonmaternal care on children." *American Psychologist, 35,* 309–319.

Etaugh, C. (1984). "Effects of maternal employment on children: An updated review." Paper presented at the annual meeting of the Midwestern Psychological Association, Chicago, IL.

Fabe, M., and Wikler, N. (1979). *Up Against the Clock: Career Women Speak on the Choice to have Children.* New York: Warner.

Frankel, J., Manogue, M.A., and Paludi, M. (1982). "The employed mother: A new social norm?" *International Journal of Women's Studies, 5,* 274–281.

Giele, J.D. (1983). "The married professional woman: An examination of her role conflicts and coping strategies." *Psychology of Women Quarterly, 7,* 235–243.

Hardesty, S.A., and Betz, N.E. (1980). "The relationships of career salience, attitudes toward women, and demographic and family characteristics to marital adjustment in dual career couples." *Journal of Vocational Behavior, 17,* 242–250.

Hoffman, L.W. (1980). "The effects of maternal employment on the academic attitudes and performance of school-aged children." *School Psychology Review, 9,* 319–335.

Lee, R.E. (1984). "When midcareer mothers first return to work. Counseling concerns." *Journal of Counseling and Development, 63,* 35–39.

Richardson, M.S. (1981). "Occupational and family roles: A neglected intersection." *The Counseling Psychologist, 9,* 5–32.

Roland, A.S., and Harris, B. (Eds.) (1979). *Career and Motherhood: Struggles for a New Identity.* New York: Human Sciences Press.

Voydanoff, P. (1980). "Work-family life cycles among women." In D. McGuigan (Ed.), *Women's Lives: New Theory, Research and Policy* (pp. 61–68). Ann Arbor, MI.: Center for Continuing Education of Women.

Watley, D.J., and Kaplan, R. (1971). "Career or marriage? Aspirations and achievements of able and young college women." *Journal of Vocational Behavior, 1,* 29–43.

Weeks, M.O., and Gage, B.A. (1984). "A comparison of the marriage-role expectations of college women: 1961-1974." *Sex Roles, 17,* 49–58.

Weitzman, L.J. (1985). *The Divorce Revolution: The Unexpected Social and Economic Consequences for Women and Children in America.* New York: Free Press.

Bibliographies, Pamphlets, and Magazines

Leavitt, J.A. (1982). *Women in Management: An Annotated Bibliography and Source List.* Phoenix: Onyx Press.

McFeeley, M.D. (1982). *Women's Work in Britain and America from the Nineties to World War I: An Annotated Bibliography.* Boston: G.K. Hall.

Faunce, P.S. (1980). *Woman and Ambition: A Bibliography.* Metuchen, NJ: Scarecrow.

"Maternity benefits in the 80s." An ILO Global Survey, 1984–1985.

Heartland: McRel Sex Equity Center Newsletter, 4709 Belleview Avenue, Kansas City, MO 64112.

Working Mother Magazine

"Federal laws and regulations prohibiting sex discrimination in educational institutions." Project on the Status and Education of Women, 1818 R Street, N.W., Washington, DC 20009.

"Summary of age discrimination Act of 1975 as contained in Title III of the Older Americans Amendments of 1975." Project on the Status and Education of Women, 1818 R Street, N.W., Washington, DC 20009.

Perry, K.S. (1982). *Employers and Child Care: Establishing Services Through the Workplace.* Women's Bureau, U.S. Department of Labor, Pamphlet 23.

Women, Education and Employment: A Bibliography of Periodical Citations, Pamphlets, Newspapers, and Government Documents, 1970–1980. Renee Feinberg, Library Professional Publications, 1982.

Women in Nontraditional Employment: A Selected List of Publications, Slides, and Films. U.S. Department of Labor, Office of the Secretary, Women's Bureau, Washington, DC.

Rothberg, D.S., and Cook, B.E. (1985). *Employee Benefits for Part-Timers.* Association of Part time professionals, Box 3419, Alexandria, VA 22303.

Organizations Concerned with Working Women

Additional information may be obtained from "A Woman's Yellow Pages," published by the Federation of Organizations for Professional Women.

Organization	Address
Women's Bureau Washington, DC 20210	U.S. Department of Labor
Federation of Organizations for Professional Women	2000 P Street, N.W. Suite 403 Washington, DC 20036
Alliance Against Sexual Coercion	P.O. Box 1 Cambridge, MA 02139
Cleveland Working Women	1258 Euclid Avenue Cleveland, OH 44115
9 to 5	YWCA 140 Clarendon Street Boston, MA 02116
Equal Employment Opportunity Commission	2401 E Street, N.W. Washington, DC 20506
National Network of Hispanic Women	P.O. Box 4223 Stanford, CA 94305
Black Career Women, Inc.	Black Career Women's Center 706 Walnut Street Suite 804 Cincinnati, OH 45202
National Commission on Working Women	2000 P Street, N.W. Suite 508 Washington, DC 20036

Audio-Visual Material

Title	Distributor	Description
Union Maids (Film)	New Day Films 22 Riverview Dr. Wayne, NJ 07470	Women reminisce about their work in organizing the C.I.O. in the late 1920s and 1930s.
Women in Sports (Film)	Pyramid Box 496 Media, PA 19063	Reviews women's participation in sports and opinions of women athletes. A discussion of Title IX is presented.
Women in Management: Threat or opportunity? (Film)	CRM/McGraw-Hill Films McGraw Hill Book Co. Delmar, CA 92014	Discusses the stereotypes associated with women in business and Affirmative Action programs.
Women in Communications (Film)	CBS 51 W. 52 Street New York, NY 10019	Looks at women's jobs in the communications media. Explores career opportunities in the communications field.
The power Pinch: Sexual Harassment in the Workplace	MTI Inc. 3710 Commercial Ave. Northbrook, IL 60062	Describes sexual harassment from the view of managers and employees.
Back to School, Back to Work (Film)	American Personnel and Guidance Association Film Department 1607 New Hampshire Ave., N.W. Washington, DC 20009	Describes women who are considering changing roles, including the stresses and difficulties in being re-entry students.
Women at Work: Change, Choice, Challenge (Film)	EBEC 425 Michigan Ave. Chicago, IL 60611	Interviews with 7 women about work and personal roles. Occupations presented: oil worker, nurse, jockey, locomotive engineer, surgeon, judge, candidate for Congress.
Women, Work, and Babies: Can America cope? (Film)	NBC 20 Rockefeller Plaza New York. NY 10020	Explores the advantages and stresses of employed mothers.

The Soviet Woman (Film)	McGraw-Hill Delmar, CA 92014	Examines the careers of motherhood, fashion modeling, student, and construction worker.
Job Interview: Whom Would you Hire? (Film)	Business Education Films 5113 16 Ave. Brooklyn, NY 11204	Describes mistakes commonly made during interviews and offers suggestions on how to correct them.
Breaking Through (Film)	Phoenix Films 468 South Avenue South New York, NY 10016	Describes a pre-trades training school that prepares women for jobs traditionally considered "masculine."
The Double Day (Film)	The Cinema Guild 1697 Broadway New York, NY 10019	Documentary about employed women in Venezuela, Mexico, Bolivia, and Argentina.
Hired Hands (Film)	California Newsreel 630 Natoma San Francisco, CA 94103	Describes secretaries' lives in terms of the duties expected of them and sexual harassment.
The Life and Times of Rosie the Riveter (Film)	Clarity Educational Productions P.O. Box 315 Franklin Lakes, NJ 07417	Documents how women were enticed by the government into blue-collar jobs that men had vacated during World War II and how they were enticed into homemaking once the men returned.

Popular Books

Title	Author/Editor	Publisher
Women on Top	J. Adams	Hawthorn
Games Mother Never Taught You	B. Harragan	Warner
And So it Goes: Adventures in Television	L. Ellerbee	Putnam
Powerplay	M. Cunningham	Linden Press
Burnout: The Cost of Caring	C. Maslach	Prentice-Hall

Guest Speakers for Presentations on Women and Work

Business and Professional Women's Organization

Career Counseling

Career Placement Center

Office of Affirmative Action

Gerontology Center

Continuing Education

Department of Vocational Education

Volunteer Organizations

Retirement Planning Services

Employment Agencies

House Care Workers

Clerical Workers

Childcare Workers

Equal Employment Opportunity Commission

Representatives From Labor Unions

Sample Discussion Questions

- Define the career clock for women. Give some examples of how it functions. Be sure to cite the turning point in the occupational cycle during the middle years.

- What is Affirmative Action? How does it work? Describe the Affirmative Action procedures at your college or place of employment.

- In recent years women's lack of a mentoring relationship has been used to explain their failure to succeed as much and/or as often as men. Citing relevant research, either support or refute this belief. Be sure to include the following issues: mixed-sex mentoring, definition of mentoring, role models *vs.* mentors, and the developmental and cultural issues in the mentor-protege relationship.

- To what extent does our society provide support for women who work outside the home in addition to working inside the home: Are these services satisfactory? What alternative procedures would you recommend?

- Cite some racial and class differences in responding to forms of sexual and gender harassment on the job.

- Why is the concept of the "superwoman" harmful for women in today's culture?

- Do you see yourself as having more than one career over your lifetime? Why or why not?

- Discuss the research on evaluations of women's performance in terms of the causal attributions employers make of women's success and failure.

- What does the research seem to suggest about women's relationships with women in the workplace?

- Does evidence exist to support the "queen bee syndrome?"

Exercise

Exercise: Dual-Wage Families

(This exercise is adapted from Matlin, 1987 and is used here with permission from Holt, Rinehart, and Winston Publishers.)

Steps for Completing the Exercise:

1. Ask students to consider the following scenario:
   Mary and Frank are two professionals who are married to each other. Currently, both of them are seeking employment. Frank has received a very good job offer and must make a decision about that job. Mary has not yet received a firm offer. However, there seems to be good possibilities for the future. Mary cannot arrange interviews before Frank's deadline. Frank may be able to locate another position in the geographic location in which Mary has possibilities.

2. Ask students to select an option from among the following alternatives:
   a. Frank accepts the job and Mary goes to look for a position in that area.
   b. Frank declines the job and they both continue to look for employment.
   c. Frank accepts the job, Mary pursues her possibilities for employment, and there is a chance that they will live separately for some period of time.

3. Place students into the three groups representing these options.

4. Ask students to list the reasons why they selected the option.

5. Have the recorder share the lists with the entire class.

6. Have a general discussion about dual-wage couples.

Exercise: Historical View of Careers

Steps for Completing the Exercise:

1. Ask students to study the roles of women in their particular future (or present) profession or career.

2. Have students trace these roles of women from an historical perspective.

3. Ask students to indicate the proportion of women in these professions.

4. Discuss how obstacles to women's success in this field may be overcome.

5. Have students indicate individual, societal, and institutional changes in order to overcome these occupational barriers.

6. Ask students what they can do to meet these goals.

7. Discuss students' alternatives.

8. Invite speakers from a variety of careers students listed to discuss the barriers as well as opportunities for women.

Exercise: Valuing Housework

Steps for Completing the Exercise:

1. Ask students to read the following job application: (from Chesler, P. (1976). *Women, Money, and Power.* New York: Bantam, p. 97.)

   Requirements: Intelligence, good health, energy, patience, sociability

   Skills: At least 12 different occupations

   Hours: 99.6 per week

   Salary: None

   Holidays: None (will be required to remain on stand-by 24 hours a day, 7 days a week)

   Opportunities for Advancement: None (limited transferability of skills acquired on the job)

   Job Security: None (trend is toward more layoffs particularly as employee approaches middle age. Severance pay will depend on the discretion of the employer.)

   Fringe Benefits: Food, clothing, and shelter generally provided, but any additional bonuses will depend on financial standing and good nature of the employer. No health, medical, or accident insurance, no social security or pension plan.

2. Discuss the diversity of responsibilities and amount of work involved in rearing children and maintaining a house.

3. Explain the amount of time that women spend on housework; discuss how this amount has not changed markedly over the years. Discuss the amount of time that men spend on housework.

4. Discuss the role strain faced by women who are employed outside the home. Indicate how this constitutes a second occupation for women.

5. Indicate how progressive cultures have failed in their attempt to eradicate gender roles because of the low status attached to housework and childrearing.

Part 6

*Victimization of Women:
Rape, Incest, Battered Women,
Gender and Sexual Harassment*

Chapter 9

Victimization of Women

Sample Outline: Gender role socialization and the victimization of women

Rape

    incidence

    theoretical views of offenders and victims

    attitudes about offenders and victims

    symptomatic impact of rape

    date rape and acquaintance rape

    marital rape

    relationship between sexuality and aggression

    relationship between pornography and aggression

    fear of rape

    counseling rape victims

    impact of rape on victim's families and friends

    rape crisis intervention

    feminist analysis of rape

    rape prevention/education/awareness

    long term adjustment of rape victims

    treatment of nonrecent rape victims

    community responses to rape

Incest

    incidence

    theoretical views of incest

    myths about incest

violence in the home

psychological aspects of incest

types of incest

long-term adjustment of incest victims

impact of incest on family system

counseling incest victims

feminist analysis of incest

Battered Women

incidence

theoretical views of battering

myths about battered women

psychological aspects of battering

impact of battering on children

long term adjustment of abused women

battering cycle

options for battered women: therapy, shelter, leaving the relationship

counseling abused women

women who murder their batterers

feminist analysis of battering

Sexual and Gender Harassment

incidence

sexual *vs.* gender harassment

explanatory models of harassment

myths about harassment victims and harassers

measurement issues

harassment in education

harassment in the workplace

view of harassment from the harassers' perspective

responses to harassment: legal, organizational, individual

counseling victims of harassment

feminist analysis of harassment

interface of racism and sexism in sexual harassment

Sample References

Rape

Bart, P., and O'Brien, P.H. (1984). "Stopping rape: Effective avoidance strategies." *Signs, 10,* 83–101.

Brownmiller, S. (1973). *Against Our Will.* New York: Simon & Schuster.

Burgess, A., and Holmstrom, L. (1974). *Rape: Victims of Crisis.* Bowie, MD: R.J. Brady.

Carter, D.L., Prentky, R., Knight, R.A., Vanderveer, R., and Boucher, R. (1987, January). "Use a pornography in the criminal and developmental histories of sexual offenders." Paper presented at the New York Academy of Sciences, New York, NY.

Holmstrom, L., and Burgess, A. (1983). *The Victim of Rape: Institutional Reactions.* New Brunswick, NJ: Transaction Books.

Koss, M.P. (1985). "The hidden rape victim: Personality, attitudinal, and situational characteristics." *Psychology of Women Quarterly, 9,* 193–212.

Koss, M.P., and Gidycz, C.A. (1985). "Sexual experiences survey: Reliability and validity." *Journal of Consulting and Clinical Psychology, 53,* 422–423.

Koss, M.P., and Harvey, M. (1987). *The Rape Victim: Clinical and Community Approaches to Treatment.* Lexington, Mass.: Stephen Greene Press.

Russell, D. (1975). *The Politics of Rape.* New York: Stein & Day.

Williams, J., and Holmes, K.A. (1981). *The Second Assault: Rape and Public Attitudes.* Westport, Conn.: Greenwood Press.

Incest

Courtois, C. (1988). *Healing the Incest Wound.* New York: Norton.

Finkelhor, D. (1979). *Sexually Victimized Children.* New York: Free Press.

Herman, J.L. (1981). *Father-Daughter Incest.* Cambridge, Mass.: Harvard University Press.

Kempe, R., and Kempe, C. (1984). *The Common Secret: Sexual Abuse of Children and Adolescents.* San Francisco: Freeman.

Rubin, R., and Byerly, G. (1983). *Incest: The Last Taboo: An Annotated Bibliography*. New York: Garland.

Rush, F. (1980). *The Best Kept Secret: Sexual Abuse of Children*. Englewood Cliffs, NJ: Prentice Hall.

Battered Women

Gelles, R.J. (1974). *The Violent Home: A Study of Psychological Aggression between Husbands and Wives*. Beverly Hills: Sage.

Howard, P.F. (1978). *Wife-Beating: A Selected, Annotated Bibliography*. San Diego: Current Bibliographic Series.

Martin, D. (1976). *Battered Wives*. San Francisco: Glide.

Nicarthy, G. (1982). *Getting Free: A Handbook for Women in Abusive Relationships*. Seattle: Seal.

Roy, M. (Ed.) (1977). *Battered Women: A Psychological Study of Domestic Violence*. New York: Van Nostrand Reinhold.

Walker, L.E. (1979). *The Battered Woman*. New York: Harper & Row.

Walker, L.E. (1979). "Battered women: Sex roles and clinical issues." *Professional Psychology, 12*, 81–91.

White, E.C. (1985). *Chain, Chain, Change*. Seattle: Seal.

Zambrano, M. (1985). *Mejor Sola que Mal Accompanada*. Seattle: Seal.

Sexual and Gender Harassment

Adams, J., Kottke, J., & Padgitt, J. (1983). "Sexual harassment of university students." *Journal of College Student Personnel, 24*, 484–490.

Benson, D., & Thompson, G. (1982). "Sexual harassment on a university campus: The confluence of authority relations, sexual interest and gender stratification." *Social Problems, 29*, 236–251.

Brodsky, C. (1976). *The Harassed Worker*. Lexington, Mass.: Lexington Books.

Cammaert, L. (1985). "How widespread is sexual harassment on campus? Special Issue: Women in groups and aggression against women." *International Journal of Women's Studies, 8*, 388–397.

Crocker, P. (1983). "An analysis of university definitions of sexual harassment." *Signs, 8*, 696–707.

Dzeich, B., & Weiner, L. (1984). *The Lecherous Professor*. Boston: Beacon Press.

Farley, L. (1978). *Sexual Shakedown*. New York: McGraw-Hill.

Fitzgerald, L., Shullman, S., Bailey, N., Richards, M., Swecker, J., Gold, Y.,

Ormerod, M., & Weitzman, L. (1988). "The incidence and dimensions of sexual harassment in academia and the workplace." *Journal of Vocational Behavior, 32,* 152–175.

Fitzgerald, L.F., Gold, Y., Ormerod, M., & Weitzman, L. (1988). "Academic harassment: Sex and denial in scholarly garb." *Psychology of Women Quarterly, 12,* 329–340.

Franklin, P., Moglin, H., Zatling-Boring, P., & Angress, R. (1981). *Sexual and Gender Harassment in the Academy.* New York: Modern Language Association.

Fuehrer, A., & Schilling, K. (1987, May). "Sexual harassment of women graduate students: The impact of institutional factors." Paper presented at the Midwestern Psychological Association, Chicago.

Glaser, R., & Thorpe, J. (1986). "Unethical intimacy: A survey of sexual contact and advances between psychology educators and female graduate students." *American Psychologist, 41,* 43–51.

Gutek, B. (1985). *Sex and the Workplace: Impact of Sexual Behavior and Harassment on Women, Men, and Organizations.* San Francisco: Jossey-Bass.

Hoffman, F. (1986). "Sexual harassment in academia: Feminist theory and institutional practice." *Harvard Educational Review, 56,* 105–121.

Hughes, J., & Sandler, B. (1986). *In Case of Sexual Harassment: A Guide for Women Students. We Hope it Doesn't Happen to You, But if it Does . . .* Washington, DC: Association of American Colleges.

Lott, B. (1982). "Sexual assault and harassment: A campus community case study." *Signs, 8,* 296–319.

McCormack, A. (1985). "The sexual harassment of students by teachers: The case of students in science." *Sex Roles, 13,* 21–32.

Padgitt, S., & Padgitt, J.S. (1986). "Cognitive structure of sexual harassment: Implications for university policy." *Journal of College Student Personnel, 27,* 34–39.

Paludi, M.A. (Ed.). (in press). *Ivory Power: Sexual Harassment on Campus.* Albany: SUNY Press.

Powell, G.N. (1986). "Effects of sex role identity and sex on definitions of sexual harassment." *Sex Roles, 14,* 9–19.

Reilly, M., Lott, B., & Gallogly, S. (1986). "Sexual harassment of university students." *Sex Roles, 15,* 333–358.

Schneider, B. (1982). "Consciousness about sexual harassment among heterosexual and lesbian women workers." *Journal of Social Issues, 38,* 75–98.

Tangri, S., Burt, M., & Johnson, L. (1982). "Sexual harassment at work: Three explanatory models." *Journal of Social Issues, 38,* 33–54.

Pamphlets, Reports, Magazines

Women Against Pornography Newsreport
359 W. 47 St.
New York, NY 10036

Sexual Harassment: A Hidden Issue
Project on the Status and Education of Women
Association of American Colleges
1818 R St., NW
Washington, DC 20009

The Problem of Rape on Campus
Project on the Status and Education of Women
Association of American Colleges
1818 R. St., NW
Washington, DC 20009

Newsletter of the Feminist Alliance Against Rape
National Communications Network for the Elimination of Violence
Against Women
Box 21003
Washington, DC 20009

What Can Students Do About Sex Discrimination?
Project on the Status and Education of Women
Association of American Colleges
1818 R St., NW
Washington, DC 20009

A Bibliography on Pornography, Rape, and Child Molestation
Women Against Pornography
358 W. 47 Street
New York, NY 10036

Freeing Our Lives: A Feminist Analysis of Rape Prevention
Women Against Rape
P.O. Box 02084
Columbus, OH 43202

Touch that Hurts: Talking with Children about Sexual Abuse
Lynne Landau
Community Advocates for Safety and Self-Reliance
4183 S.E. Division
Portland, OR 97202

Organizations Concerned with the Victimization of Women

National Center for the Prevention and Control of Rape
National Institute of Mental Health
5600 Fishers Lane
Rockville, MD 20857

Rape Crisis Center
917 15th St.
Washington, DC 20009

Women Against Rape
Women's Action Collective
P.O. Box 02084
Columbus, OH 43202

National Clearinghouse for the Defense of Battered Women
Suite 302
125 South 9th St.
Philadelphia, PA 19107

Child Sexual Abuse Prevention Project
Office of the County Attorney
2000-C Hennepin Government Center
Minneapolis, MN 55487

Montana Incest Prevention Coalition
315 S. 4th St.
Missoula, MT 59801

Emerge
25 Huntington Avenue
Room 324
Boston, MA 02116

Family Violence Research and Treatment Program
University of Texas at Tyler
3900 University Blvd.
Tyler, TX 75701

Community Program Against Sexual Assault
100 Warren St.
Roxbury, MA 02119

Alliance Against Sexual Coercion
P.O. Box 1
Cambridge, MA 02139

9 to 5
  YWCA
  149 Clarendon St.
Boston, MA 02116

Stop Sexual Abuse of Children
  Chicago Public Education Project
  American Friends Service Committee
  407 South Dearborn St.
  Chicago, IL 60605

Project on the Status and Education of Women
  1818 R St., NW
  Washington, DC 20009

Organizations that Have Worked on the Issue of Pornography

Women Against Pornography
  358 W. 47 St.
  New York, NY 10036

Women Against Violence Against Women
  543 North Fairfax Avenue
  Los Angeles, CA 90036

Women Against Violence in Pornography and Media
  P.O. Box 14635
  San Francisco, CA 94114

Audio-Visual Material

Title	*Distributor*	*Description*
	RAPE	
Rape: Face to Face (Film)	Filmakers Library 124 E. 40th St. New York, NY 10016	Interviews with rape survivors, rapists, and counselors.
Why Men Rape (Film)	Learning Corporation of America 420 Academy Dr. Northbrook, IL 60015	Documentary about rapists.
Not Only Strangers presentation (Film)	Centron P.O. Box 687 Lawrence, KS 66044	Dramatized account of a rape survivor.
Acquaintance Rape Prevention (Films)	ODN Productions 114 Spring St. New York, NY 10012	Films deal with power issues involved in rape.
Not a Love Story (Film)	National Film Board of Canada 1251 Avenue of the Americas New York, NY 10010	Describes the impact of pornography on physical violence against women.
Rape Culture (Film)	Cambridge Documentary P.O. Box 285 Cambridge, MA 02139	Illustrates the role of societal forces in promoting rape.
Rape/Crisis (Film)	The Cinema Guild 1697 Broadway New York, NY 10019	Discusses the aftermath of rape and the work of a rape crisis center.
	INCEST	
Breaking Silence (Film)	Film Distribution Center 1028 Industry Dr. Seattle, WA 98193	Describes incest victims' discussions of their victimization with therapists and family members.
Incest: The Family Secret (Film)	Filmakers Library 124 E. 40th St. New York, NY 10016	Interviews with a father who had incestuous relationships with his daughter and mothers who were aware of the victimization.

BATTERED WOMEN

Battered Wives (Film)	Michael Jaffe Learning Corporation of America 420 Academy Dr. Northbrook, IL 60015	Interviews with women and men concerning the emotional and physical aspects of violence against women.
Battered Women: Violence Behind Closed Doors (Film)	MTI Teleprograms 3710 Commercial Ave. Northbrook, IL 60662	Addresses assistance provided by police, shelters, and counselors.
Loved, Honoured, and Bruised (Film)	Media Guild 11526 Sorento Valley San Diego, CA 92121	Interviews with an abused wife and her husband reveal the power issues involved in the abusive relationship.

SEXUAL AND GENDER HARASSMENT

You are the Game: Sexual Harassment on Campus (Film)	Indiana University Audio-Visual Center Bloomington, IN 47405	Documents sexual and gender harassment of college women; panel discussion with scholars.
Workplace Hustle (Film)	Clark Communications 943 Howard St. San Francisco, CA 94103	Interviews with women who have been harassed.
The Willmar 8 (Film)	California Newsreel 630 Natoma St. San Francisco, CA 94103	Discusses women who went on strike because of sex discrimination.
The Power Pinch (Film)	MTI Teleprograms 3710 Commercial Ave. Northbrook, IL 60062	Describes harassment in the workplace.

Popular Books

Title	Author	Publisher
Father's Days	K. Brady	Dell
The Color Purple	A. Walker	Pocket
Silent Children A Book for Parents about Child Abuse	L. Sanfor	Doubleday
The Women's Room	M. French	Jove
Scream Quietly or the Neighbors Will Hear	E. Pizzey	Enslow
I Know Why the Caged Bird Sings	M. Angelou	Bantam
I Never Called it Rape	R. Warshaw	Harper & Row
Professor Romeo	A. Bernays	Weidenfeld & Nicolson
Against our Will	S. Brownmiller	Simon & Schuster

Guest Speakers for Presentations on Victimization of Women

University Counseling Center

Rape Crisis Center

Equal Employment Opportunity Commission

Women's Shelter

Affirmative Action Office

University/College Attorney

9 to 5

National Organization for Women

Business and Professional Women's Association

Assault Crisis Center

Sample Discussion Questions

- Contrast the term "rape victim" with the term "rape survivor." What do the terms convey in relationship to women's strength and power?

- Discuss the convergence of sexism and racism in terms of predicting feminist definitions of harassment, battering, rape, and incest situations and willingness to prosecute individuals for these acts.

- Discuss some reasons for college women not labeling their victimization experiences as victimization.

- Describe the research by Mary Koss and her colleagues on date and acquaintance rape.

- How do you think college and university campuses should deal with sexual and gender harassment?

- Discuss feminist therapeutic approaches to women who have experienced forms of victimization.

- Discuss Lenore Walker's work with battered women.

- Describe the results obtained by David Finkelhor with regard to the incidence of incest.

- Describe how sexual assault by men against girls and women is related to women's status in their culture.

- Discuss the literature on women who fight back and kill their attackers.

- Offer some community interventions for physically abused women.

- Discuss the research by Edward Donnerstein, who has reported that exposure to pornography has demonstrable effects on men's attitudes and behavior toward women.

Exercises

Exercise

Assertiveness in our Lives

(This exercise is adapted from one by Andrea Parrot and is used here with her permission.)

Steps for Completing the Exercise:

1. Introduce the session by using a nonthreatening example which relates to assertiveness but does not also carry along with it the discomfort associated with a discussion of sexuality. This is an example which relates to smoking in an elevator. Tell participants the following:
   a. You are all nonsmokers for the duration of this example. You hate cigarette smoke.
   b. You are waiting for an elevator on the first floor, and you must ride to the third floor. When it arrives you get on it and so does someone with a lit cigarette.
   c. WHAT DO YOU DO/ (Try to elicit as many different responses as possible from the participants).
   d. WOULD YOUR RESPONSE BE DIFFERENT IF THERE WAS A "NO SMOKING" SIGN IN THE ELEVATOR?
   e. WOULD YOUR RESPONSE BE DIFFERENT IF THIS PERSON WERE YOUR SUPERVISOR OR TEACHER?
   f. WOULD YOUR RESPONSE BE DIFFERENT IF SMOKING IN ELEVA-TORS WERE ILLEGAL?

2. The responses probably ranged from very nonassertive (such as I would hold my breath, or I would get off the elevator and walk), to aggressive (such as cigarettes are disgusting, or I would put it out for him of her), to lying (such as I am allergic to cigarette smoke). Did the types of responses differ by sex? If so why?

In most likelihood, very few of the examples were assertive, and would not fit into the formula of: "When you do 'x', I feel 'y'". Assertions are difficult with people we do not know, but may even be more difficult with people we know.

3. Explain that there are several reasons why it is even more difficult to be assertive in a sexual interaction:
   a. You must put your desires over those of someone you care about when you are asserting for something contrary to the desires of others.
   b. You are not usually taught or encouraged to talk about sex or use sexual words in normal conversation.

213

c. Communication about sex often takes place in the context of "game playing," not honest communication about feelings.
d. We are not generally expected to share our feelings with others, especially if that sharing may make us vulnerable.
e. We may not be absolutely sure about what we want sexually.
f. We have been receiving conflicting messages from many different sources in our lives about what is correct and how we should behave sexually.
g. We can use the law or our health as reasons to assert for our dislike of someone else smoking around us, because smoking may be hazardous to health and is illegal in some nonventilated public areas. We cannot use the law or physical health to defend against our discomfort with behaviors such as "petting."
h. Either men or women are allowed to dislike smoking, but neither sex is supposed to dislike sex, and each sex is bound by certain restrictive sex roles.

Exercise: Community Centers Assisting Women

Steps for Completing the Exercise:

1. Ask students, in groups of 5–10, to inquire about the number and variety of community mental health centers in their college or university community. Assign one group the topic of rape crisis centers, another to battered women's shelters, etc.

2. Have students pick two centers and interview an employee or volunteer about the services provided by the center.

3. Ask students to provide the address of the center, its purpose, and the name of the person they interviewed (with permission).

4. Provide this material to all the students in the class. Ask the students to post the information in their residence halls, religious community, etc.

5. Invite one or two of the interviewed individuals to participate in class. You may want to open up the class to students from other classes.

Exercise: Sexual and Gender Harassment of Students

Steps for Completing the Exercise:

1. Describe the impact of sexual and gender harassment on students' career aspirations and perceptions of self-worth.

2. Discuss myths about harassment:
   - harassment only affects a few women
   - harassment is rare on campus
   - women should ignore harassment when it occurs
   - most charges of sexual harassment are false
   - harassment is sexual joking

3. Define sexual and gender harassment.

4. Discuss sexual harassment and the law.

5. Describe how colleges and universities deal with complaints of sexual harassment.

6. Ask students to obtain a copy of their university's or college's policy on sexual harassment.

7. Ask students to write out the steps they would take in seeking redress from harassment.

8. Ask students to describe the short-term and long-term consequences for each step they describe.

9. Have the students share their responses in a group of 10–15 other students.

10. Ask each small group to summarize their strategies and issues raised.

11. Allow each group to share their responses with the rest of the class.

12. Offer suggestions of organizations which have worked on the issue of sexual harassment.

Part 7

Interpersonal Relationships

Chapter 10

Verbal and Nonverbal Communication

Sample Outline

Language: Quantitative and qualitative aspects

Elements of gender differences in verbal communication

    lexical disparities

    differential use of expletives

    syntactic disparities

    adjectives denoting admiration *vs.* description

    disclaimers

    intonational patterns

    tag questions

    intensifiers

    imperatives

Perceptions about "male" and "female" speech: Implications for careers

    Gender differences in language: Power explanations

    Self-disclosure

    Linguistic sexism

    ignoring women

    defining women

    deprecating women

Nonsexist language

Male as normative

Men and women as conversational partners

    interruptions

    overlaps

    verbosity

    topics

    listening

Nonverbal cues of status: Gestures of dominance and submission

    touching

    smiling

    laughing

    personal space

    eye contact

    body position and posture

Sample References

Verbal Communication

Blaubergs, M.S. (1978). "Changing the sexist language: The theory behind the practice." *Psychology of Women Quarterly, 2,* 244–261.

Bradley, P.H. (1981). "The folk-linguistics of women's speech: An empirical examination." *Communication Monographs, 45,* 1–17.

Cook, A.S., Fritz, J.J., McCormack, B.L., and Visperas, C. (1985). "Early gender differences in the functional usage of language." *Sex Roles, 9,* 909–915.

Derlega, V.J., Durham, B., Gockel, B., and Shollis, D. (1981). "Sex differences in self-disclosure: Effects of topic content, friendship, and partner's sex." *Sex Roles, 7,* 433–447.

Elshtain, J. (1982). "Feminist discourse and its discontents: Language, power, and meaning." *Signs, 7,* 603–631.

Haas, A. (1979). "Male and female spoken language differences: Stereotypes and evidence." *Psychological Bulletin, 86,* 616–626.

Haas, A. (1981). "Partner influences on sex-associated spoken language of children." *Sex Roles, 7,* 925–935.

Hyde, J.S. (1984). "Children's understanding of sexist language." *Developmental Psychology, 20,* 697–706.

Key, M.R. (1975). *Male/Female Language.* Metuchen, NJ: Scarecrow Press.

Kramer, C. (1974, June). "Folk-linguistics: Wishy-washy mommy talk." *Psychology Today,* 82–89.

Kramer, C., Thorne, B., and Henley, N. (1978). "Perspectives on language and communication." *Signs, 3,* 638–651.

Lakoff, R. (1975). *Language and Women's Place.* New York: Harper & Row.

Pearson, J. (1985). *Gender and Communication.* Dubuque: William C. Brown.

Rasmussen, J.L., and Moley, B.E. (1986). "Impression formation as a function of the sex role appropriateness of linguistic behavior." *Sex Roles, 14,* 149–161.

Siderits, M., Johannsen, W., and Fadden, T. (1985). "Gender, role, and power: A content analysis of speech." *Psychology of Women Quarterly, 9,* 439–450.

Sleight, C., and Prinz, P. (1982). "Children's color vocabulary." *Language and Speech, 25,* 75–79.

Stericker, A. (1981). "Does this "her or she" business really make a difference? The effects of masculine pronouns as generics on job attitudes." *Sex Roles, 7,* 627–642.

Thorne, B., and Henley, N. (Eds.) (1975). *Language and Sex: Differences and Dominance.* Rowley, MA: Newbury House.

Wiley, M., and Eskilson, A. (1985). "Speech style, gender stereotypes, and corporate success: What if women talk more like men?" *Sex Roles, 9,* 993–1007.

Nonverbal Communication

Berman, P.W., and Smith, V.L. (1984). "Gender and differences in children's smiles, touch, and proxemics." *Sex Roles, 10,* 347–356.

Brabant, S., and Mooney, L. (1986). "Sex role stereotyping in the Sunday comics: Ten years later." *Sex Roles, 14,* 141–148.

Bull, P. (1983). *Body Movement and Interpersonal Communication.* New York: Wiley.

Hall, J.A. (1978). "Gender effects in decoding nonverbal cues." *Psychological Bulletin, 85,* 845–857.

Hall, J.A., and Halberstadt, A.G. (1981). "Sex roles and nonverbal communication skills." *Sex Roles, 1,* 273–287.

Henley, N. (1977). *Body Politics: Power, Sex, and Nonverbal Communication.* Englewood Cliffs, NJ: Prentice-Hall.

Juni, S., and Bremon, R. (1981). "Interpersonal touching as a function of status and sex." *Journal of Social Psychology, 114,* 135–136.

LaFrance, M. (1981). "Gender gestures: Sex, sex-role, and nonverbal communication." In C. Mayo and N. Henley (Eds.), *Gender and Nonverbal Behavior*. New York: Springer-Verlag.

Lombardo, W.K., Cretser, G.A., Lombardo, B., and Mathis, S.L. (1983). "Fer cryin' out loud—There is a sex differences." *Sex Roles, 9,* 987–995.

Mayo, C., and Henley, N. (Eds.) (1981). *Gender and Nonverbal Behavior.* New York: Springer-Verlag.

Ragan, J.H. (1982). "Gender displays in photographs." *Sex Roles, 8,* 33–44.

Rossi, S.R., and Rossi, J.S. (1985). "Gender differences in the perception of women in magazine advertising." *Sex Roles, 12,* 1033–1039.

Saunders, C.S., and Stead, B.A. (1986). "Women's adoption of a business uniform: A content analysis of magazine advertisements." *Sex Roles, 15,* 197–205.

Shakin, M., Shakin, D., and Sternglanz, S.H. (1985). "Infant clothing: Sex labeling for strangers." *Sex Roles, 9,* 955–964.

Silverstein, B., Perdue, L., Peterson, B., and Kelly, E. (1986). "The role of the mass media in promoting a thin standard of bodily attractiveness for women." *Sex Roles, 14,* 519–532.

Wiemann, J., and Harrison, R. (Eds.) (1983). *Nonverbal Interaction.* Beverly Hills, Calif.: Sage.

Pamphlets and Bibliographies

Jarrard, M.E.W., and Randall, P.R. (1982). *Women Speaking: An Annotated Bibliography of Verbal and Nonverbal Communication, 1970–1980.* New York: Garland.

Lee, R. (Ed.). *The Guide to Nonsexist Language and Visuals.* University of Wisconsin Bookstore, 432 North Lake Street, Madison, WI 53706.

Audio-Visual Material

Title	Distributor	Description
Killing us Softly (Film)	Cambridge Documentary Films Box 385 Cambridge, MA 02139	Description of sexism in advertising.
Gender Based Language (Film)	WBGU-TV Bowling Green State University Bowling Green, OH 43403	Ways to eliminate sexist language.
Calling the Shots (Film)	Cambridge Documentary Films P.O. Box 385 Cambridge, MA 02139	Advertising of alcohol and the way in which the ads appeal to addicts.

Popular Books

Title	Author/Editor	Publisher
Male/Female Language	M.R. Key	Scarecrow
Body Language	J. Fast	Pocket
Language and Women's Place	R. Lakoff	Harper & Row
Body Language of Children	P. Szasz	Morrow

Guest Speakers for Presentations on Verbal and Nonverbal Communication

Speech Communication

Speech Pathology and Audiology

Department of Rhetoric and Communication

Speech and Hearing Clinic

Department of English

Audio-Visual Services

Graphics Production

News Service

Newspaper

Radio and Television Information Services

Sign Language Expert

Teleproductions

Advertising Department

Sample Discussion Questions

- Discuss how and why men and women using identical linguistic features are perceived differently.

- Describe cultural issues involved in verbal and nonverbal communication.

- Discuss how women's verbal and nonverbal communication may be viewed positively in work and relationship settings.

- Describe developmental discontinuities in verbal and nonverbal communication patterns.

- Discuss positive implications of the use of tag questions, *e.g.*, encouraging more conversation with one's partner.

- Jot down how many times you smile when the issue doesn't require a smile or laugh. Why do you think women smile even when they are not happy?

- Look through a high school yearbook. Jot down the number of women who are smiling. Do the same for the men. Why do you think women use this form of nonverbal communication more than do men?

- Describe the ways you can use nonsexist language in your everyday interactions.

Exercise

Exercise

Role Reversal in Women-Men Communication Styles
    (Adapted from A.G. Sargent (Ed.) (1985). *Beyond Sex Roles*. New York: West, and is used with permission).

Steps for Completing the Exercise:

1. Break up the class into smaller groups, each containing 3–4 men and women.

2. Select a topic for discussion. You may want to use the information presented in this unit on verbal and nonverbal communication.

3. Have each group select a recorder who will note verbal and nonverbal communication patterns. You may want to have two recorders: one male; one female. You could then compare their descriptions.

4. Ask the men to follow traditional guidelines for women's communication style. Ask them to:
   a. Be deferential—don't interrupt;
   b. After making a point in the conversation, laugh or let your voices trail off in some discounting manner;
   c. Smile a lot;
   d. Look at the other group members alot, particularly (in this case) the women for approval.

5. Ask women to follow traditional guidelines for men's communication style. Ask them to:
   a. Be assertive;
   b. Interrupt others if they don't complete their thought quickly enough for you;
   c. Talk in paragraphs;
   d. Ignore nonverbal cues;
   e. Don't look at anyone in particular when you talk.

6. Have each group discuss the topic for 10–15 minutes.

7. Ask the recorders to share their observations with the entire class.

9. Discuss nonsexist communication styles.

For example:

Blaubergs, M.S. (1978). "Changing the sexist language: The theory behind the practice." *Psychology of Women Quarterly, 2,* 244–261.

American Psychological Association (1975). "Task force on issues of sexual bias in graduate education. Guidelines for nonsexist use of language." *American Psychologist, 30,* 682–684.

Exercise: Male as Normative

Steps for Completing the Exercise:

1. Ask students to read a newspaper or magazine article (with an accompanying photograph) and discuss the direct and indirect messages about men and women.

2. Ask students to reverse the pronouns and reread the article with the modifications.

3. Have students compare and contrast the messages about men and women before and after the modifications.

4. Ask students to discuss the nonverbal symbols present in the photograph: smiling, personal space, fashion, eye contact, etc. What message is being conveyed to the reader?

5. Have students display their articles and photographs in the classroom; allow students the opportunity to view each of these.

6. Have a general discussion about the imagery and symbolism in the definition of women and men.

Exercise

Women's Speak *vs.* Men's Speak

The idea for this exercise is credited to Christine Sleight. It is used here with her permission.

Steps for Completing the Exercise:

1. Prepare a list of words and phrases (examples are given below) to show to the students in the class.
   Sample Items
   ecru

nice
on pins and needles
ain't
darling
runnin'
about
perpetrator
hitting below the belt
read
adorable
hammer
caregiver

2. Ask students to indicate the words and phrases they believe are typically used by men.

3. Ask students to indicate the terms they believe are typically used by women.

4. Ask students comment on their evaluations and whether the sex of the evaluator plays an important part in this process.

Exercise: Nonverbal Gestures of Power

The idea for this exercise is credited to Christine Sleight. It is used here with her permission.

Steps for Completing the Exercise:

1. Have students observe three or four mixed-sex pairs in their dorm, classroom, etc.

2. Ask students to record the following:
   how often the women touch the men
   how often the men touch the women
   whether one individual of each pair moves toward and/or away from the other one

3. Have students bring their observations to class. Determine whether or not the sex of the observer plays an important role in this process.

Exercise: Nonsexist Language Usage

Steps for Completing the Exercise:

1. Ask students to break up into smaller groups; assign a recorder for each group.

2. Distribute a list of terms similar to the following:
   sportsmanship
   stewardess
   chairman
   businessman
   mankind
   manhole cover
   policeman
   fireman
   policewoman
   penmanship

3. Ask each group to generate nonsexist alternatives to these terms.

4. Distribute sexist sentences similar to the following:
   Julie is such a little tomboy.
   John is such a sissy.
   I expect you girls to act like ladies in this class and you boys better be gentlemen.
   The men's basketball team and the girl's basketball team won last night.
   I like the dancers and the male dancers too.
   We have slimnastics here for girls and body building for boys.
   He throws like a girl.
   Let's have four-man teams.

5. Ask each group to write a nonsexist alternative to each sentence.

6. Ask the recorders to share with the entire class the alternatives that their groups generated.

7. Discuss the implications of nonsexist language in textbooks and children's readers.

Source:

McGraw-Hill Book Company (1974). *Guidelines for Equal Treatment of the Sexes in McGraw-Hill Book Company Publications.* New York: McGraw Hill.

Chapter 11

Women and Sexuality

Sample Outline

Women's sexual anatomy

Women's physiology of sexual response

Women's sexual desires

Sex education

Communicating about sex

Sexual activities

Masturbation

Responses to erotic stimuli

Virginity

Lesbian relationships

Bisexual relationships

Celibacy

Older women and sexuality

Sex and physical disabilities

Sexual dysfunction

   unresponsiveness

   orgasmic dysfunction

   vaginsmus

   dippareunia

Therapy for sexual dysfunction

Birth control

Abortion

Sexual health care

Sexuality *vs.* sexual behavior

Politics of sex

Sample References

Women's Sexual Anatomy and Physiology of Sexual Responses

Belzer, E. (1981). "Orgasmic expulsions of women: A review and heuristic inquiry." *Journal of Sex Research, 17,* 1–12.

Boston Women's Health Book Collective (1984). *The New Our Bodies, Ourselves.* New York: Simon & Schuster.

Hyde, J.S. (1983). *Understanding Human Sexuality.* New York: McGraw-Hill.

Masters, W., and Johnson, V. (1966). *Human Sexual Response.* Boston: Little Brown.

Perry, J., and Whipple, B. (1981). "Pelvic muscle strength of female ejaculators: Evidence in support of a new theory of orgasm." *Journal of Sex Research, 17,* 222–39.

Radlove, S. (1983). "Sexual response and gender roles." In E. Allgeier and N. McCormick (Eds.), *Changing Boundaries.* (pp. 87–103). Palo Alto: Mayfield.

Vance, E., and Wagner, N. (1977). "Written descriptions of orgasm: A study of sex differences." In D. Byrne and L. Byrne (Eds.), *Exploring Human Sexuality.* (pp. 201–222). New York: Crowell.

Women's Sexual Desires

Blumstein, P., and Schwartz, P. (1983). *American Couples.* New York: William Morrow.

Gold, A., and Adams, D. (1981). "Motivational factors affecting fluctuations of female-sexual activity at menstruation." *Psychology of Women Quarterly, 5,* 670–680.

Hite, S. (1976). *The Hite Report.* New York: Dell.

Hite, S. (1987). *Women and Love.* New York: St. Martin's Press.

Morokoff, P. (1988). "Sexuality in perimenopausal and postmenopausal women." *Psychology of Women Quarterly, 12,* 489–511.

Quante, A.L. (1981, April). "Attitudes toward sexually assertive women." Paper presented at the meeting of the Eastern Psychological Association, New York, NY.

Vance, C.S. (Ed.) (1984). *Pleasure and Danger: Exploring Female Sexuality.* Boston: Routledge & Kegan Paul.

Sex Education

Dreyer, P.H. (1982). "Sexuality during adolescence." In B.B. Wolman (Ed.), *Handbook of Developmental Psychology.* (pp. 559–601). Englewood Cliffs, NJ: Prentice Hall.

Fox, G., and Inazu, J. (1980). "Mother-daughter communication about sex." *Family Relations, 29,* 347–352.

Katz, J., and Cronin, D. (1983). "Sexuality and college life." In O. Pocs (Ed.), *Human Sexuality 83/84)* (pp. 25–30). Guildord, Conn.: Dushkin.

Zellman, G.L., and Goodchilds, J.D. (1983). "Becoming sexual in adolescence." In E. Allgeier and N. McCormick (Eds.), *Changing Boundaries.* (pp. 49–63). Palo Alto: Mayfield.

Lesbian Relationships (See also Chapter on Personal Choices and Social Scripts)

Blumstein, P., and Schwartz, P. (1983). *American Couples.* New York: William Morrow.

Coleman, E. (1982). "Developmental stages in the coming out process." *Journal of Homosexuality, 7,* 31–43.

Espin, O. (1987). "Issues of identity in the psychology of Latina lesbians." In Boston Lesbian Psychologies Collective (Eds.), *Lesbian Psychologies: Explorations and Challenges.* Champaign, IL: University of Illinois Press.

Peplau, L.A., and Amaro, H. (1982). "Understanding lesbian relationships." In W. Paul, J. Weinrich, J. Gonsiorek, and M. Hotvedt (Eds.), *Homosexuality: Social, Psychological, and Biological Issues.* (pp. 233–247). Beverly Hills: Sage.

Roberts, J.R. (1981). *Black Lesbians.* Boston: Hall.

Schneider, M.S. (1986). "The relationships of cohabitating lesbian and heterosexual couples: A comparison." *Psychology of Women Quarterly, 10,* 234–239.

Tanner, D. (1978) *The Lesbian Couple.* Lexington: Lexington Books.

Sex and Physical Disabilities

Becker, E.F. (1978). *Female Sexuality Following Spinal Cord Injury.* Bloomington, IL: Cheevar.

Bullard, D., and Knight, S. (Eds.) (1981). *Sexuality and Disability: Personal Perspectives.* St. Louis: Mosby.

Duffy, Y. (1981). *All Things are Possible.* Ann Arbor: Garvin.

Sexuality of Older Women

Allgeier, E.R. (1983). "Sexuality and gender roles in the second half of life." In E. Allgeier and N. McCormick (Eds.), *Changing Boundaries.* (pp. 135–157). Palo Alto: Mayfield.

Datan, N., and Rodeheaver, D. (1983). "Beyond generativity: Toward a sensuality of later life." In R. B. Weg (Ed.), *Sexuality in the Later Years.* (pp. 279–288).

Pocs, O., Godow, A., Tolone, W.L., and Walsh, R. (1983). "Is there sex after 40?" In O. Pocs (Ed.), *Human Sexuality 83/84.* (pp. 190–192). Guildor, CT: Dushkin.

Weg, R. (Ed.) (1983). *Sexuality in the Later Years.* New York: Academic Press.

Sexual Dysfunction

Anderson, B.L. (1983). "Primary orgasmic dysfunction: Diagnostic considerations and review of treatment." *Psychological Bulletin, 93,* 105–136.

Nichols, M. (1982). "The treatment of inhibited sexual desire in lesbian couples." *Women and Therapy, 1,* 49–66.

Pogrebin, L.C. (1983). "Nonsexist sexuality." In G. Albeem, S. Gordon, and H. Leitenberg (Eds.), *Promoting Sexual Responsibility and Preventing Sexual Problems.* (pp. 66–95). Hanover, NJ: University Press of New England.

Schwartz, P., and Strom, D. (1978). "The social psychology of female sexuality." In J. Sherman and F. Denmark (Eds.), *Psychology of Women: Future Directions of Research.* New York: Psychological Dimensions.

Tevlin, H., and Leiblum, S. (1983). "Sex role stereotypes and female sexual dysfunction." In V. Franks and E. Rothblum (Eds.), *The Stereotyping of Women: Its Effects on Mental Health.* (pp. 129–150). New York: Springer-Verlag.

Birth Control

Adler, N. (1981). "Sex roles and unwanted pregnancy in adolescent and adult women." *Professional Psychology, 12,* 56–66.

Allgeier, E. (1983). "Reproduction, roles, and responsibilities." In E. Allgeier and N. McCormick (Eds.), *Changing Boundaries.* (pp. 163–181).

Byrne, D. (1979). "Determinants of contraceptive values and practices." In M. Cook and G. Wilson (Eds.), *Love and Attraction.* (pp. 301–307). Oxford, England: Pergamon.

Gerrard, M., McCann, L., and Geis, B.D. (1984). "Antecedents and prevention of unwanted pregnancy." In A. Rickel, M. Gerrard, and I. Iscoe (Eds.), *Social and Psychological Problems of Women: Prevention and Crisis Intervention.* Washington, DC: Hemisphere.

Abortion

Adler, N., and Dolcini, P. (1986). "Psychological issues in abortion for adolescents." In G.B. Melton (Ed.) *Adolescent Abortion: Psychological and Legal Issues.* Lincoln: University of Nebraska Press.

Belovitch, T.E. (1980). "The experience of abortion." In C. Heckerman (Ed.), *The Evolving Female.* (pp. 92–106). New York: Human Sciences.

Bishop, N. (1984). "Abortion: The controversial choice." In J. Freeman (Ed.), *Women: A Feminist Perspective.* (pp. 39–53). Palo Alto: Mayfield.

Combs, M., and Welch, S. (1982). "Blacks, Whites, and attitudes toward abortions." *Public Opinion Quarterly, 46,* 510–520.

David, H.P., and Matejcek, Z. (1981). "Children born to women denied abortion: An update." *Family Planning Perspectives, 13,* 32–34.

Henshaw, S., Binkin, N., Blaine, E., and Smith, J. (1985). "A portrait of American women who obtain abortions." *Family Planning Perspectives, 17,* 90–96.

Petchesky, R. (1984). *Abortion and Women's Choice: The State, Sexuality, and Reproductive Freedom.* New York: Longman.

Washington, A. (1982). "A cultural and historical perspective on pregnancy-related activity among U.S. teenagers." *Journal of Black Psychology, 9,* 1–28.

Pamphlets and Periodicals

Chico Feminist Women's Health Center
330 Flume St.
Chico, CA 95926

The Facts about VD
Los Datos Sobre EV
Copies in English and Spanish
Department of Public Health
Division of Communicable Disease
600 Washington St.
Boston, MA 02111

Worried About VD
It's a Fact of Life—VD Gets Around
New York State Health Department
Office of Communications and Educations
Tower Building
Empire State Plaza
Albany, NY 12237

Lesbian Health Matters
Herpes
Santa Cruz Women's Health Center
250 Locust St.
Santa Cruz, CA 95060

The Helper: Quarterly Newsletter of the Herpes Resource Center
P.O. Box 100
Palo Alto, CA 94302

Sexually Transmitted Diseases
Quarterly Publication of the American Venereal Disease Association
P.O. Box 200
San Diego, CA 92134

Sexually Transmitted Diseases
Abstracts and Bibliography
Center for Disease Control
Bureau of State Services
Atlanta, GA 30333

STD Newsletter
City of New York
Bureau of Venereal Disease Control
New York City Health Department
93 Worth St.
Room 806
New York, NY 10013

Organizations Concerned with Women and Sexuality

Organization	*Address*
American Association of Sex Educators, Counselors, and Therapists	11 Dupont Circle Suite 220 Washington, DC 20036
Sex Information and Education Council of the U.S.	84 Fifth Avenue New York, NY 10011
National Women's Health Network	224 Seventh St. Washington, DC 20003
Information Service of the Kinsey Institute for Sex Research	416 Morrison Hall Indiana University Bloomington, IN 47401
National Gay Task Force	80 Fifth Avenue New York, NY 10011
Feminist Self-Insemination Group	Albion Yard Building K, 17 a Balfe St. London N1 9ED, England
STD Helpline	415-388-7710
VD Helpline	800-227-8922
In California:	800-982-5883
Committee for Abortion Rights and Against Sterilization Abuse	17 Murray St. New York, NY 10007

Audio-Visual Material

Title	Distributor	Description
VD and Women (Video)	Perennial Education 477 Roger Williams Highland Park, IL 60035	Description of herpes and gonorrhea.
Personal Decisions (Film)	The Cinema Guild 1697 Broadway New York, NY 10019	Discusses women's rights to control their reproductive lives.
Abortion: Stories from North and South (Film)	The Cinema Guild 1697 Broadway New York, NY 10019	Cross-cultural information about abortion.
Facts About Sexually Transmitted Disease (Film)	Benchmark Films 145 Scarborough Rd. Briarcliff Manor, NY 10510	Description of several kinds of STDs.
Homosexuality and Lesbianism (Video)	The Cinema Guild 1697 Broadway New York, NY 10019	Addresses concerns and fears about gay lifestyles.
After the Game (Film)	Focus International, Inc. 333 W. 52 St. New York, NY 10019	Discusses a lesbian relationship.
When Teens Get Pregnant (Film)	Polymorph Films 118 South St. Boston, MA 02111	Adolescents discuss their pregnancies and care of infants.
The Ultimate Test Animal (Video)	The Cinema Guild 1697 Broadway New York, NY 10019	Examines Depo Provera.
So Many Voices: A Look at Abortion (Film)	Phoenix Films 468 Park Avenue South New York, NY 10016	Interviews with women whose mothers died of illegal abortions.
Silent Pioneers: Gay and Lesbian Elders (Film)	Filmakers Library 124 E. 40th St. New York, NY 10016	Focuses on elderly lesbians and gay men.

236

Popular Books

Title	Author/Editor	Publisher
The Hite Report	S. Hite	Dell
The New Celibacy	G. Brown	McGraw-Hill
The Family Book about Sexuality	M. Calderone and E. Johnson	Bantam
Shared Intimacies: Women's Sexual Experiences	L. Barbach and L. Levine	Bantam
For Yourself: The Fulfillment of Female Sexuality	L. Barbach	Doubleday
Sexual Scripts	J. Laws and P. Schwartz	University Press of America
Women, Sex, and Sexuality	C. Stimpson and E. Person	University of Chicago Press
Women's Sexual Experience: Explorations of the Dark Continent	M. Kirkpatrick	Plenum
Sex for Women Who Want to Have Fun and Loving Relationships with Equals	C. Kerr	Grove press
The Illustrated Manual of Sex Therapy	H. Kaplan	New York Times Book Company
Sexuality and Disability: Personal Perspectives	D. Bullard and S. Knight	C. V. Mosby

Guest Speakers for Presentations on Women and Sexuality

Department of Physiology

Department of Psychology

Public Health Nurse

School of Nursing

Behavioral Medicine

Registered Nurses Association

Sex Therapist

American Association of Sex Educators, Counselors, and Therapists

Sex Information and Educational Council of the United States

Planned Parenthood

Abortion Clinic

Clergy

Gynecologist

Political Scientist

Sample Discussion Questions

A good sourcebook that contains exercises for a unit on women and sexuality is the Instructor's Manual to Accompany Janet Hyde's text on Human Sexuality.

- Discuss the double bind posed for adolescent women who are expected to the sexy but not sexual.

- Describe the double standard of sexuality with respect to number of sexual partners and initiation of sexual relationships.

- Discuss some stereotypes about women's sexuality. How are these stereotypes perpetuated by the media?

- Outline the information you would present to an adolescent woman about women's sexuality. What topics would you include? Which, if any, would you omit? Why?

- How have feminist researchers changed the androcentric nature of the study of sexuality?

- Why is information about lesbian relationships and bisexual relationships typically omitted from discussions of women's sexuality?

- Discuss some cross-cultural research on the practice and perceptions of abortion.

- Describe the kinds of sexually transmitted diseases. How would you discuss this information with an adolescent woman?

- Offer some explanations for the high incidence of teenage pregnancies among women who were aware of birth control methods but decided to not use any or require their partner to use any.

- What information should be discussed in high school sex education classes about the emotional aspects of a relationship?

- Discuss some of the problems faced by elderly lesbian women in terms of society's acceptance of their lifestyles.

- Offer some explanations for the popularity of radio and television talk-shows (with phone-ins) dealing with sexuality, *e.g.*, The Dr. Ruth Westheimer show.

Exercises

Exercise

Sexuality and Sex Education

Steps for Completing the Exercise:

1. Ask students to answer for themselves the questions presented in the accompanying table.

2. Have students establish discussion priorities.

3. Post responses to the top two questions from the survey items.

4. Ask the class to form a fishbowl(s) with an outer group and an inner group.

5. Leave one or two empty chairs in the inner circle. Those students in the outer circle who have something to say can be allowed to enter the inner circle and take part. They leave the inner circle when they believe they have exhausted their input.

6. Allow the inner group to discuss the responses to the survey items for 10–15 minutes.

7. Allow 10–15 minutes at the end for students in the outer group to make comments.

8. Post the major conclusions that are drawn from the discussion of sex education for adolescents.

Source:

Zellman, G.L., and Goodchilds, J.D. (1983). "Becoming sexual in adolescence." In E.R. Allgeier and N.B. McCormick (Eds.), *Changing Boundaries* (pp. 49–63). Palo Alto: Mayfield.

Table of Questions Related to Sexuality and Sex Education

1. From which sources (*e.g.*, parents, siblings, peers, teachers, books) did you learn about sexuality?

2. Do you believe you received adequate and accurate information?

3. Was the emotional side of sexuality discussed with you?

4. Was (were) your parent(s) comfortable about discussing sexuality?

5. Did you receive information about gay relationships and lesbian relationships?

6. From whom did you learn about contraception, abortion, sexual dysfunctions? Was this information adequate and accurate?

Exercise

Media Portrayal of Older Women's Sexuality

Steps for Completing the Exercise:

1. Ask students to watch 3–4 movies or television programs depicting older women.

2. Ask students to indicate whether these women are portrayed as sensuous and sexual.

3. Compare students' responses with the entire class.

4. Present research indicating older women's sexual capacity and performance in post-menopausal years.

   Source:

   Pocs, O., Godow, A., Tolone, W., and Walsh, R. (1983). "Is there sex after 40?" In O. Pocs (Ed.), *Human Sexuality.* (pp. 190–192). Guildord, Conn.: Dushkin.

   Allgeier, E.R. (1983). "Sexuality and gender roles in the second half of life." In E.R. Allgeier and N.B. McCormick (Eds.), *Changing Boundaries* (pp. 135–157). Palo Alto, Mayfield.

5. Facilitate a general discussion of sexuality and older women. Be sure to include the following issues:

   decline in estrogen production at menopause

   vagina's loss of elasticity

lack of a sexual partner in older adulthood

double standard of sexuality for men and women in older adulthood

Exercise: Methods of Birth Control

Steps for Completing the Exercise:

1. Ask students to list what they believe are the methods of birth control available, their effectiveness and side effects.

2. Post students' responses on the board.

3. Be sure students list birth control methods intended for men as well as for women.

   Source:

   Stewart, F., Guest, F., Stewart, G., and Hatcher, R. (1981). *My Body, My Health*. New York: Bantam.

Methods to mention:

natural family planning

abstinence

withdrawal

spermicidal foam

diaphragm

condoms

intrauterine device

birth control pills

cervical cap

vasectomy

tubal ligation

contraceptive sponge

4. Discuss why most of the birth control methods are intended for women. Issues to highlight: reproductive cycles, pregnancy, contraceptives developed by men.

5. Distinguish between women controlling their own reproductive capacities and total responsibility for birth control until menopause.

6. You may want to invite an individual from Planned Parenthood to participate in the discussion.

Topics to discuss:

who uses birth control

reasons for not using birth control

religious issues surrounding birth control use

media denial of contraceptive use

inadequate and inaccurate information about birth control

sex education

Exercise: Media Portrayal of Lesbian Women

Steps for Completing the Exercise:

1. Ask students to view 2–3 comedy programs and/or variety shows.

2. Have student record the number of antilesbian jokes and remarks told in the programs.

3. Ask students to comment on the jokes mentioned. Post these responses for the entire class.

4. Analyze the comments in terms of stereotypes of lesbian women.

5. Ask students to discuss how they would feel if they were lesbians and heard these comments.

6. Discuss the research on lesbian women's relationships and homophobia people have.

Source:

Peplau, L.A., and Amaro, H. (1982). "Understanding lesbian relationships." In W. Paul, J.D. Weinrich, J.C. Gonsiorek, and M.E. Hotvedt (Eds.), *Homosexuality: Social, Psychological, and Biological Issues* (pp. 233–247). Beverly Hills: Sage.

Boston Lesbian Psychologies Collective (Eds.) (1988). *Lesbian Psychologies: Explorations and Challenges.* Champaign, IL: University of Illinois Press.

Chapter 12

Personal Choices and Social Scripts

Sample Outline

Families in historical perspective

World revolutions and family patterns

Processes of the family

Motherhood mandate

Child effects on parents

Parenthood and adult development

Sibling relationships

Variations in family styles

   single-parent families

   singlehood

   nonmarital heterosexual cohabitation

   voluntary childlessness

   lesbian relationships

   blended families

   adoptive parents

   celibacy

   bisexual relationships

   commuter marriages

   dual wage families

   divorce

   widowhood

Issues in personal choice

legal and public policy issues

religious issues and reactions to variations in family styles

Families in distress

child abuse

physical violence in families

runaways and throwaways

Sample References

Voluntary Childlessness

Benedick, E., and Vaugh, R. (1982). "Voluntary childlessness." In M. Kirkpatrick (Ed.), *Women's Sexual Experiences.* (pp. 205–222). New York: Plenum.

Campbell, F.L., Townes, B.D., and Beach, L.R. (1982). "Motivational bases of childbearing decisions." In G.L. Fox (Ed.), *The Childbearing Decision.* (pp. 145–159). Beverly Hills: Sage.

Faux, M. (1984). *Childless by Choice: Choosing Childlessness in the 80s.* New York: Doubleday.

Houseknecht, S. (1978). "Voluntary childlessness: A social psychological model." *Alternative Lifestyles, 1,* 379–402.

Veevers, J. (1973). "Voluntary childlessness." *Sociology and Social Research, 57,* 356–366.

Employed Mothers, Family Context, and Day Care

Anderson-Kulman, R.E., and Paludi, M.A. (1986). "Working mothers and the family context: Predicting positive coping." *Journal of Vocational Behavior, 28,* 241–253.

Beckman, L.J., and Houser, B.B. (1979). "The more you have, the more you do: The relationships between wife's employment, sex-role attitudes, and household behavior." *Psychology of Women Quarterly, 4,* 160–174.

Etaugh, C. (1984, May). "Effects of maternal employment on children: An updated review." Paper presented at the Midwestern Psychological Association, Chicago, IL.

Gray, J. (1983). "The married professional woman: An examination of her role conflicts and coping strategies." *Psychology of Women Quarterly, 7,* 235–243.

Hardesty, S.A., and Betz, N. (1980). "The relationships of career salience, attitudes toward women, and demographic and family characteristics to marital adjustment in dual career couples." *Journal of Vocational Behavior, 17,* 242–250.

Hoffman, L.W. (1989). "Effects of maternal employment in the two-parent family." *American Psychologist, 44,* 283–292.

Zigler, E., and Muenchow, S. (1983). "Infant day care and infant care leaves." *American Psychologist,* 91–94.

Friendships

Abbey, A. (1982). "Sex differences in attributions for friendly behavior: Do males misperceive females' friendliness?" *Journal of Personality and Social Psychology, 42,* 830–838.

Aries, E., and Johnson, F. (1983). "Close friendship in adulthood: Conversational content between same-sex friends." *Sex Roles, 9,* 1183–1196.

Bell, R.R. (1981). "Friendships of women and of men." *Psychology of Women Quarterly, 5,* 402–417.

Caldwell, M.A., and Peplau, L.A. (1982). "Sex differences in same-sex friendship." *Sex Roles, 8,* 721–732.

Davidson, S., and Packard, T. (1981). "The therapeutic value of friendship between women." *Psychology of Women Quarterly, 5,* 495–510.

Rose, S. (1985). "Same-sex and cross-sex friendships and the psychology of homosociality." *Sex Roles, 12,* 63–74.

Multiple Roles and Role Strain

Gilbert, L., and Gram, A. (1984, August). "Parental satisfaction and responsibilities in dual-earner and traditional families: Are there differences?" Paper presented at the American Psychological Association, Toronto, CN.

Gilbert, L., Holahan, C., and Manning, L. (1981). "Coping with conflict between professional and maternal roles." *Family Relations, 30,* 419–426.

Harrison, A., and Minor, J.H. (1983). "Interrole conflict, coping strategies, and role satisfaction among single and employed mothers." *Psychology of Women Quarterly, 6,* 334–360.

Delayed Parenting

DeVore, N.E. (Ed.) (1983). "Parenthood postponed." *American Journal of Nursing,* 83.

Frankel, S., and Wise, J. (1982). "A view of delayed parenting: Some implications of a new trend." *Psychiatry, 45,* 220–225.

Bisexual Women

Blumstein, P., and Schwartz, P. (1977). "Bisexuality: Some social psychological issues." *Journal of Social Issues, 33,* 30–45.

Klein, F. (1976). *The Bisexual Option: A Concept of One Hundred Percent Intimacy.* New York: Arbor House.

LaTorre, R., and Wendenburg, K. (1983). "Psychological characteristics of bisexual, heterosexual, and homosexual women." *Journal of Homosexuality, 9,* 87–97.

Lesbian Women (See also chapter on Sexuality)

Hill, M. (1987). "Child rearing attitudes of Black lesbian mothers." In Boston Lesbian Psychologies Collective (Eds.), *Lesbian Psychologies: Explorations and Challenges.* Champaign, IL: University of Illinois Press.

Kirkpatrick, M., Smith, C., and Row, R. (1981). "Lesbian mothers and their children." *American Journal of Orthopsychiatry, 51,* 545–551.

Martin, D., and Lyon, P. (1985). "The realities of lesbianism." In J. Williams (Ed.), *Psychology of Women.* New York: Norton.

Pagelow, M. (1980). "Heterosexual and lesbian single mothers." *Journal of Homosexuality, 3,* 189–204.

Peplau, L.A., Padesky, C., and Hamilton, M. (1982). "Satisfaction in lesbian relationships." *Journal of Homosexuality, 8,* 23–35.

Wolf, D. (1979). *The Lesbian Community.* Berkeley: University of California Press.

Heterosexual Relationships

Cunningham, J.D., and Antill, J.K. (1984). "Changes in masculinity and femininity across the family life cycle: A reexamination." *Developmental Psychology, 20,* 1135–1141.

Deaux, K., and Hanna, R. (1984). "Courtship in the personals column: The influence of gender and sexual orientation." *Sex Roles, 11,* 363–375.

Denmark, F., Shaw, J., and Ciali, S. (1985). "The relationship among sex roles, living arrangements, and the division of household responsibilities." *Sex Roles, 12,* 617–625.

Hill, C., Peplau, L.A., and Rubin, A. (1981). "Differing perceptions in dating couples: Sex roles *vs.* alternative explanations." *Psychology of Women Quarterly, 5,* 418–434.

Peplau, L.A. (1984). "Power in dating relationships." In J. Freeman (Ed.), *Women: A Feminist Perspective.* Palo Alto: Mayfield.

Risman, B., Hill, C., Rubin, Z., and Peplau, L. (1981). "Living together in college: Implications for courtship." *Journal of Marriage and the Family, 43,* 77–83.

Rubin, Z., Peplau, L., and Hill, C. (1981). "Loving and leaving; Sex differences in romantic attachments." *Sex Roles, 7,* 821–835.

List of Organizations Offering Resources for Children Being Raised in a Non-Nuclear Family

American Library Association
Committee on the Status of Women
50 Easy Huron Street
Chicago, IL 60611

Change for Children
2588 Mission St.
Room 226
San Francisco, CA 94110

Children's Book Council
175 Fifth Avenue
New York, NY 10010

Feminist Press
311 East 94 St.
New York, NY 10128

Lollipop Power
P.O. Box 1171
Chapel Hill, NC 27514

Ms. Magazine
370 Lexington Avenue
New York, NY 10017

Women on Words and Images
P.O. Box 2163
Princeton, NJ 08540

National Organization for Women
425 13 St., NW
Suite 1048
Washington, DC 20004

Organizations Concerned with Personal Choices and Social Scripts

National Single Parent Coalition
225 Park Avenue
New York, NY 10003

Parents Without Partners
7910 Woodmont Avenue
Bethesda, MD 20814

Single Mothers By Choice
Box 7783 FDR Station
New York, NY 10150

Stepfamily Association of America
284 Allegheny Avenue
Baltimore, MD 21204

Stepfamily Foundation
333 West End Avenue
New York, NY 10023

Remarried Parents
102-20 67 Drive
Forest Hills, NY 11375

Children of Gays/Lesbians
691 South Irold Street
Los Angeles, CA 90003

National Association for the Childless
Birmingham Settlement
318 Summer Lane
Birmingham, England BL9 3 RL

Custody Action for Lesbian Mothers
P.O. Box 281
Narberth, PA 19072

Lesbian Mothers' Union
339 Ellis Street
San Francisco, CA 94102

Senior Action in a Gay Environment
208 West 13 Street
New York, NY 10011

Lesbian Rights Project
1370 Mission Street
San Francisco, CA 94103

Federation of Parents and Friends of Lesbians and Gays
    Box 24565
    Los Angeles, CA 90024

Disabled Lesbian Alliance
    Room 229
    5 University Place
    New York, NY 10003

American Adoption Congress
    P.O. Box 23641
    Washington, DC 20004

Audio-Visual Material

Title	Distributor	Description
Silent Pioneers: Gay and Lesbian Elders (Film)	Filmakers' Library 124 E. 40th St. New York, NY 10016	Discusses stereotypes and realities about gay and lesbian lifestyles.
39, Single, and Pregnant (Film)	Filmakers' Library 124 E. 40th St. New York, NY 10016	Describes advantages of late parenting and single parenting.
Delayed Parenthood: Pros and Cons (Film)	CBS, Inc. 51 W. 52nd St. New York, NY 10019	Describes career decisions, economic demands and medical advances that influence women's decisions to delay parenthood.
And Baby Makes Three (Film)	Filmakers' Library 124 E. 40th St. New York, NY 10016	Describes joys and stresses of parenting in a White and a Black family.
Choosing Children (Film)	Cambridge Documentary Films P.O. Box 385 Cambridge, MA 02139	Discusses lesbian women who become parents through a variety of methods.
In The Best Interests of the Children (Film)	Iris Feminist Collective Box 5353 Berkeley, CA 94705	Describes the relationships between lesbian women and their children.
Back To School, Back To Work (Film)	American Personnel and Guidance Film Department 1607 New Hampshire Ave., NW Washington, DC 20009	Describes women who are considering a change in roles.

Careers and Babies (Film)	Polymorph Films 118 South St. Boston, MA 02111	Women discuss the relationship between career and family life.
Joyce at 34 (Film)	New Day Films 22 Riverview Drive Wayne, NJ 07470	Discussion of late parenting.
Who Remembers Mama? (Film)	New Day Films 22 Riverview Drive Wayne, NJ 07470	Discussion of displaced homemakers.
Nana, Mom, and Me (Film)	New Day Films 22 Riverview Drive Wayne, NJ 07470	Describes intergenerational relationships among women.
One, Two, Three, Zero: Infertility (Film)	Filmakers' Library 124 E. 40th St. New York, NY 10016	Discussion of fertility clinic.

Popular Books

Title	Author/Editor	Publisher
The Color Purple	A. Walker	Pocket
Lesbian Poetry: An Anthology	E. Bulkin and J. Larkin	Persephone
Learning to Leave:	L. Triere	Warner
Man Child: A Black Lesbian Feminist's Response	A. Lorde	Conditions: Four (article)
Intimate Strangers	L. Rubin	Harper & Row
Rocking the Cradle: Lesbian Mothers—A Challenge in Family Living	G.E. Hanscombe and J. Foster	Alyson
Mothers on Trial: The Battle for Children and Custody	P. Chesler	McGraw-Hill
The Ever Single Woman	N. Peterson	Quill
The Two Paycheck Marriage	C. Bird	Pocket
Lesbian Relationship Handbook	P. Athey and M. Kinheart	Kinheart

Knock Wood	C. Bergen	Simon & Schuster
Options	F. Bright	Pocket
Rubyfruit Jungle	R.M. Brown	Bantam
A Passion for Friends: Toward a Philosophy of Female Affection	J. Raymond	Beacon
Of Woman Born: Motherhood as Experience and Institution	A. Rich	Norton
How to be a Couple and Still be Free	T. Tessina and R. Smith	Newcastle
Considering Parenthood: A Workbook for Lesbians	C. Pies	Spinsters
Our Lives for Ourselves: Women who have Never Married	N. Peterson	Putnam
The Politics of Housework	E. Malos	Schocken
American Couples	P. Bluemstein and P. Schwartz	Pocket

Guest Speakers for Presentations on Personal Choices and Social Scripts

    Department of Sociology

    Department of Anthropology

    American Civil Liberties Union

    Parents Without Partners

    Midwives

    Nannies

    La Leche League

    Obstetrician

    Daycare Center Staff

    National Association for the Childless

    Planned Parenthood

    American Association of Sex Educators

    Attorney for Lesbian Rights

    Child Custody Attorney

Sample Discussion Questions

- Gloria Steinem has stated that women tend to identify themselves as "creatures of economic necessity and familial devotion." Discuss this statement in terms of the politics of motherhood.

- Describe the ways women who reject the wife and/or motherhood mandate are discriminated against in terms of work, family relationships, schools, neighborhoods, and the media.

- Phyllis Schafly has exclaimed "why should a man marry a woman who refuses to be a mother to his children when he can get everything else he wants from women at a price much cheaper than marriage?" Is motherhood a mandate women are required to fulfill? Is having children usually viewed as a justification of female existence?

- Judith Bardwick once noted that the typical pattern of friendships between girls alternates between intimacy and repudiation. Discuss how this pattern sets a stage of mistrust of girls and women.

- Discuss the research on employed mothers and the impact of their working on their young children's cognitive and emotional development.

- Discuss the impact of on-site day care centers on employed women and their families, work productivity, and the child.

- Discuss the similarities in dealing with the loss of a relationship that divorced women and widowed women face.

- Describe several nursery rhymes or fairy tales you were told and/or read that describe relationships. What direct and indirect messages does this rhyme or tale convey about women's trustworthiness, morality, friendships with women, sexuality, relationships with parent(s)?

- Discuss the research concerning lesbian relationships in terms of coping strategies and issues of power.

- Cite several examples of cultural distinctiveness issues in personal choices and social scripts.

Exercises

Exercice

Role Strain and Conflict in Re-Entry Women Who are Mothers
 Steps for Completing the Exercise:

1. Ask the women in the class who have children to form the inner group of a fishbowl. The rest of the class may form the outer group.

2. Ask the inner group to discuss issues concerning being a student and mother. Sample discussion topics include:

   sources of role conflict

   assistance (*e.g.*, household cleaning) received from mates and other family members

   coping strategies

3. Allow 10–15 minutes for the women in the inner group to discuss the topics. Assign a recorder to take notes from the discussion.

4. Allow 6–8 minutes at the end of those students in the outer group to make comments.

5. Post the major conclusions that are drawn from the discussion.

6. Discuss with the class the impact of role strain on women's lives. Describe the outcomes of role conflict between pursuing a career and family responsibilities: fatigue, emotional depletion, guilt.

7. Cite research that suggests children of employed mothers are not cognitively or socially deprived.

Exercise

Cultural Pressures for Dating
 Steps for Completing the Exercise:

1. Discuss the literature concerning ambiguous messages about the importance of heterosexual relationships in women's lives. Describe the research indicating that many adolescent women are told by their parent(s) and peer group that their most important goal is to attract and keep a man.

Source:

Komarovsky, M. (1982). "Female freshman view their future: Career salience and its correlates." *Sex Roles, 8,* 299–314.

2. Ask students to complete a dating-rating checklist. One fun and interesting one consists of the advertisements in the personals columns of *City Newspaper,* Rochester, New York. It was developed by Margaret Matlin (1987) and in used here in abbreviated form with permission from Holt, Rinehart, and Winston.

---

1. I'd like to meet a (   ) who likes doing the same things that I enjoy doing (dancing, going out to bars occasionally, etc.).

2. I am looking for a well-rounded (   ) who can be honest, fair, and enjoy many of the interests that I have listed.

3. Wanted! A clean cut, medium built 25–33 year old (   ) who likes nature hikes early in the morning.

4. Boat owner, looking for (   ) mate, age 35–42, to share summer of boating fun.

---

3. Ask students to answer whether these statements are true or false for themselves.

4. Determine whether there are any ethnic and racial distinctiveness.

5. Ask students to suggest the ways peer pressures affect their perceptions of characteristics that are essential for a date or mate.

6. Discuss the research on women who "deviate" from the norm in relationships; *e.g.,* lesbian women, single women.

7. Ask students to describe the attitudes toward women in these two groups.

Sources:

Etaugh, C., and Malstrom, J. (1981). "The effect of marital status on person perception." *Journal of Marriage and the Family, 43,* 801–805.

Lowewnstein, S., Bloch, N., Campion, J., Epstein, J., Gale, P., and Salvatore, M. (1981). "A study of satisfaction and stresses of single women in midlife." *Sex Roles, 7,* 1127–1141.

Exercise

Attitudes Toward Childless Women

This exercise is adapted from Margaret Matlin (1987) and is used here with permission from Holt, Rinehart, and Winston.

Steps for Completing the Exercise:

1. Divide the class into two large groups.

2. Distribute one of the two versions of the material presented below to each group.

3. Distribute copies of the rating sheet presented below. Ask the student to rate their impression of Robin. Have the students do this rating individually then as a group.

4. Post the groups' average responses for all items. How is Robin portrayed if she chooses or does not choose to have children?

5. Note any gender, racial, ethnic differences and similarities in responses.

6. Discuss the research on reactions to women who don't want to have children.

Source:

Knaub, P.K., Eversoll, D., and Voss, J. (1983). "Is parenthood a desirable adult role? An assessment of attitudes held by contemporary women." *Sex Roles, 9,* 355–362.

Campbell, E. (1986). *The Childless Marriage: An Exploratory Study of Couples who do not Want Children.* New York: Tavistock.

––

Passage A:

Robin is 25 years old and is a social worker with a county agency. She finds the work challenging and gratifying, though it does have its frustrating aspects. For two years now, she has been married to Jim, who teaches high school social studies. Robin and Jim consider themselves to be happily married and they enjoy being with each other very much. Robin and Jim have decided not to have any children. They enjoy going to movies and getting together with friends and they also like to play tennis.

Passage B:

For the sentence "Robin and Jim have decided not to have children," substitute the sentence, "Robin and Jim would like to have two children."

——

Rating Scale:

Rate Robin on the following personality characteristics. Let 1 stand for "almost always true of Robin;" let 7 stand for "almost never true of Robin."

Characteristics:

well adjusted

unstable

unfriendly

warm

selfish

loving

stable

insensitive

immature

unloving

unselfish

mature

adjusted